The New Dynamic Communication Skills Handbook for Women

Second Edition

9 Steps to Effective and Professional Communication Skills for Today's Successful Business Woman

Edited by National Press Publications

NATIONAL PRESS PUBLICATIONS
A Division of Rockhurst University Continuing Education Center, Inc.
6901 West 63rd Street • P.O. Box 2949 • Shawnee Mission, Kansas 66201-1349
1-800-258-7248 • 1-913-432-7757

The New Dynamic Communication Skills Handbook for Women:
9 Steps to Effective and Professional Communication Skills for
Today's Successful Business Woman

Published by National Press Publications, Inc.
Copyright 2000 National Press Publications, Inc.
A Division of Rockhurst University Continuing Education Center, Inc.

All rights reserved. No part of this publication may be reproduced or utilized in any form by any means, electronic or mechanical, including photocopying, recording or by any information storage and retrieval systems, without permission in writing from National Press Publications.

Printed in the United States of America

1 2 3 4 5 6 7 8 9 10

ISBN 1-55852-266-2

Table of Contents

Introduction v

1 "She" Says — "He" Says 1
    Who Said That? 2

2 Assertive Communication 19
    The Benefits of Assertive Behavior 20
    Steps to Assertiveness 22
    The Assertive Message 25
    Understand That You Have the Right to Say "No" Without
    Feeling Guilty 26

3 Is Anybody Listening? 33
    Four Truths About Listening 33
    Active Listening 34

4 Nonverbals: The Unspoken Language of Communication 43
    Believe It First 44
    The Way We Communicate 45

**5 Handling the Big Four — Conflict, Crisis, Criticism
and Compliments** 61
    Conflict 61
    Crisis 69
    Criticism 72
    Compliments 77

6 Effective Writing 87
    Is Writing the Best Medium? 87
    Know What You Want to Say 89
    Who Are Your Readers, and How Should They Be Addressed? 90
    Effective Writing 94
    How to Say It Correctly 95

7   Telephone Techniques..**97**
　Telephone Negatives 97
　Three Ways to Win the Telephone Battle 98
　Thirty Tips for Effective Telephone Usage 99

8   Dynamic Presentations..**103**
　Public Speaking Is Stressful 103
　Ten Factors for Making a Dynamic Presentation 104
　Preparation Pointers 106

9   The Next Step..**113**
　The Good News Gets Better 113
　Building Your Edge 116
　The Final Word 117

Index **123**

INTRODUCTION

A lack of skill can damage your career! Most people would agree with that statement from a career counselor. After all, it's pretty basic advice to polish the skills that will ensure success.

Many of us have heard the complaint from our colleagues or even caught ourselves saying things like, "I trained hard for my job, but all I seem to do is try to fix people problems." These kinds of people skills are what we mean by communication skills. Often, they are the very skills we didn't learn! Since we all communicate in one way or another from birth, we tend to conclude that we don't need to learn how to do it at all. Like walking, it just happens. However, like power walking differs from strolling around the mall, business communication is not at all like chatting with a friend over coffee.

Women are especially vulnerable to presenting a distorted image to others through their communication style. The very attributes that enable a woman to work well with others, build relationships, seek consensus and empathize and persuade might work against her when she tries to climb the corporate ladder. Many senior managers are still very much bound by the mores of the old, white-male establishment. Not only do they expect leaders to communicate their way, but they become uncomfortable when the communicator is female. This is unfortunate, unfair and unacceptable but must be recognized as true.

Finding ways to communicate effectively, while maintaining your unique strengths as a woman in business is a skill you must learn and develop. As with all skills, it takes time and practice. But the first step, as always when we face a new challenge, is to recognize our need, assess our strengths and begin working on the areas where we need to grow the most first.

Despite the shift into the 21st century, we are and probably will continue to be hampered by the past for some time to come. Women have made great advances in the workplace, but many areas remain to be conquered. Girls are still taught differently from boys. Passive, manipulative, deferential and nurturing styles of behavior are considered appropriate for girls; aggressive, competitive, boastful and demanding styles are permitted for boys. Girls tend to play in small groups, suggesting activities and taking turns. Boys play in larger groups, impose rules and follow leaders' orders. They compete, value winning and want to be best.

Men are still viewed as doing valuable, paid work. Women are still seen as caregivers whose work is not paid for and therefore not valuable. These attitudes will not vanish overnight although they are gradually softening and will eventually change. You might feel angry and frustrated about it, but the fact remains and must be faced.

The task for women in business today is to recognize the worth of what they have and build upon it. Scrapping the strengths you already possess and trying to be something you aren't won't work. A quick look at the last few paragraphs will show that many of the things that little girls do as they play closely reflect the consensual style of today's business environment, especially in middle management. That probably explains why there are more female than male middle managers in American companies today.

The aim of this book is to help you:

- Make those female strengths work for you by learning how to apply them to your work.

- Adapt male communication skills, which are highly valued in top management, to enable others to see you as a leader.

INTRODUCTION

- Avoid the aggressive label while using assertive, authoritative language that others will respect.

- Become aware of nonverbals that might betray insecurities that your words are trying to conceal and might blur the meaning of your message.

- Learn to listen well. (Listening is often described as a feminine strength, but very few people of either sex know just how valuable this communication skill can be when it is properly applied.)

- Handle some of the especially tricky situations such as dispute-solving or accepting compliments without losing your professionalism.

- Keep your professional image intact while communicating via the telephone or the written word. Consistency and honesty are important to maintaining the image you want others to see when they look at you. Face-to-face communication is only a part of the communication picture.

> *"There are two ways of meeting difficulties.*
> *You alter the difficulties or you alter yourself to meet them."*
> Phyllis Bottome

Finally, remember that the glass ceiling does exist. It's still hard for women to get into those coveted top managerial jobs. Make sure that you're not the one preventing yourself from achieving the goal of success you've set. Don't let poor communication skills hamper your climb to the top of the corporate ladder.

1 "SHE" SAYS — "HE" SAYS

Hector and Maria were deep in discussion about the project assigned to their team. Hector was behind schedule on his report, and as his supervisor, Maria wanted to make sure that Hector understood what was needed to complete his part of the work.

"I think it would be very good if you could take just a little more time out of some of the other things you're doing — although I don't mean to imply that those other things aren't also important — and perhaps concentrate just a little bit more on getting the report finished," Maria told him.

"I want to finish up on the Simpson file first," replied Hector.

"Yes, well, the Simpson file certainly needs some work, too," Maria agreed hastily, "but, I think, although you may not agree with me, that the project report is terribly important. I'd like it done soon." She ended her last sentence on an up note that made it sound like a question that Hector could respond to.

"There isn't time to do both of them," said Hector firmly.

"Would you like more time?" asked Maria, trying to be helpful.

DYNAMIC COMMUNICATION SKILLS FOR WOMEN

Who Said That?

Here's a quick quiz to test your ear for those word-choice differences that turn communication into a gender issue.

Place an F or an M after each of the following statements to indicate whether She or He is doing the talking.

Check your responses with the answer key.

1. "The best way to tackle the problem is to get the facts on paper first." _____
2. "Take my word for it, that will not fit in this space." _____
3. "We'll go for the earliest date, OK?" _____
4. "This whole situation is a mess; what are you doing about it?" _____
5. "My professor told us to use Grigg's Method." _____
6. "Isn't it just the teeniest bit too wide?" _____
7. "Have the report on my desk by noon tomorrow." _____
8. "I have the feeling we'd do better if we tried my idea." _____
9. "Things look kind of bad. How can I help to put it right?" _____
10. "I've found Humbolt's Hypothesis to be sound." _____
11. "I can't go because my car is making a weird sound, and I have to get it fixed." _____
12. "We'll have it for you in two weeks." _____
13. "Would you have time to make 30 copies of the report for the board members?" _____
14. "I have a conflicting appointment." _____

"SHE" SAYS — "HE" SAYS

SHE SAID:	HE SAID:
Statements #	Statements #
3	1
5	2
6	4
8	7
9	10
11	12
13	14

Even if you never make a single one of those telltale statements, you probably had little difficulty in recognizing the gender differences they display. If you did recognize some of your own statements, this book will help you begin to catch the communication slip-ups that give others an image of you that you probably don't want them to have.

These female statements reflect communication styles that lead others to believe that you lack assertiveness and self-confidence. They can make you appear passive, uncertain and indecisive, lacking in the leadership qualities that will advance your career.

If you are unsure of how you sound to others, listen to yourself. Leave a miniature tape recorder near your desk for a few hours and surprise yourself when you play it back. Even listening to the messages you place on voice mail can be quite revealing.

Habits of speech are deeply rooted and might be harder to change than you first realize. Get into the habit of thinking before you speak. One of the traits that women often display is a tendency to rush into speech to cover an awkward silence or avoid conflict. Silence can be a powerful tool for a strong business leader. If you tend to speak too hastily without thinking, you might lay yourself open to making errors, getting off the topic or giving away valuable information.

Here are some of the other communication no-no's that appeared in the quiz and that undermine the professional woman's credibility and authority.

Women Say It Like a Question

- A rising inflection at the end of a sentence will make you sound as if you are asking a question even if you do not tack an interrogative such as "OK?" on to the end of your statement.

- Women actually ask about three times as many questions as men do and will even say things they know perfectly well in question form.

- Both men and women tend to believe what a man tells them in a factual, flat-out way.

- Men tend to question and interrupt when a woman makes a presentation. This might be because women can sound less sure of what they are saying.

Men feel positive about asking questions to get clarification. The tentative, questioning style of speaking that women often use might be creating doubt about what they say. It is as if women who do this are submitting their ideas for approval before believing them themselves.

Keep the voice tone down at the end of a sentence so that any statement you make comes out as a finished product, rather than a topic for adjustment, amendment or debate. Your advantage here is that when you truly are unsure, you will be more able to admit it and seek assistance than your male counterparts. There is strength in a willingness to learn that many decisive individuals lack.

Delegating and assigning tasks need to be done decisively. Using a questioning tone or seeking corroboration when handing out assignments will cause confusion about roles, deadlines and responsibilities. If you have trouble sounding decisive, try writing your orders down so that you can eliminate the

"She" Says — "He" Says

tentative, questioning words that creep into your speech. Use e-mail or memos for a while until you feel you can sound as authoritative in person as you do in writing. In our opening scenario with Maria and Hector, think how much more effective Maria could have been if she'd written down exactly what she wanted Hector to do.

Women Use a Lot of Adjectives and Adverbs

Words that hedge an otherwise assertive statement undermine the professional image we want to present. We know what should be done, but we add another's opinion to bolster our own. We might use words such as "kind of" or "maybe" to soften the statement.

In an effort to appear more assertive, we use "very," "incredibly" and "fabulous," as if our audience needs more than the facts to accept what we are trying to convey.

The unspoken, or metamessage — one that usually speaks louder than the words we say — is that we fear that our statement is unlikely to convince, so reinforcements are needed to get it across.

> Maria decided to speak to Hector again. This time, she tried to be more forceful. She met him in the hallway and said, "Gosh, Hector, I'm sorry, but your project report seems to be still kinda late, doesn't it?"
>
> Hector looked surprised. "What do you mean?" he asked her.

Adjectives and adverbs give color and warmth to speech. They establish the individuality, style and personality of the speaker. People who deal only in plain facts can seem cold and boring. In the past, business leaders have frequently valued a cold and boring business manner. Although attitudes are changing, we still tend to find cold, hard facts more convincing than flowery speeches even in the modern business world.

Get some help from a friend on this one. It can be hard to spot your foibles so ask a friend to critique your speech for an hour. What are your pet adjectives? Knowing them will help you check yourself when you pop one into a sentence at work.

Find a formula that will help you say things that you say frequently without adding the hedge or qualifier. This is especially important when asking for work to be done. At first you will feel you are being rude or brusque, but it will get easier. And the funny thing is, people will probably pay more attention to your statement and mend their ways, so you could end up never having to say it again.

Women Apologize and Explain

There is nothing wrong with saying you are sorry, if you made a mistake.

However, take a look at the example of hedging we used in the previous section. Now, how often have you heard someone make it even worse by saying "Oh gosh, Mary, I'm sorry, but this assignment seems kinda late"? Not only is the speaker hedging, but she is taking the blame for the problem. Refusing to take ownership of someone else's problem is one of the major steps toward becoming more assertive. Do not apologize for the other person's mistake. State the problem and wait, in silence, for them to apologize and explain.

When you need to explain yourself, keep it short. One of the pitfalls for women is a tendency to say too much. Nowhere does this show up more than when it comes to explaining. If this problem is yours, you probably cringe at the memory of pouring out your whole life history and present social situation in an effort to avoid working late on your birthday. Your boss's eyes glazed over, and everyone else sidled out of the office while you went on and on.

Men seldom get caught in this communication trap. Simply saying you cannot work overtime because of a prior engagement is all the explanation needed. If you're on informal terms with your boss, then by all means tell her you are being taken out to dinner for your birthday but be aware that such explanations are unnecessary and often unwarranted in a business setting.

"She" Says — "He" Says

Making excuses is something subordinates do to avoid punishment by superiors. If you want to apologize assertively, then the best method is to take responsibility and redo it right.

> When Maria's boss questioned her about the delay in the final project report, she said, "Gee, I'm so sorry, I know it's late, and believe me, I really didn't expect the delay, but I hope you'll forgive me this one time since it really wasn't planned, and I know that I should have kept on top of the subreports, but it's been so busy in my department, and I couldn't put in the overtime I usually do since I have to take my son to his remedial reading classes, and I did try to get the subreports in, but everyone is so busy right now it's hard to get them to see the importance of being on time, and I'm really very, very sorry."

Rather than apologize and overexplain, Maria could say, "I'm sorry there was a delay in the project report. I've taken steps to ensure it won't happen again."

Leaders take responsibility for their teams. If you're a supervisor, and your department makes a mistake, you're responsible. It's not good business to blame subordinates.

- Deal with the errors within the group.
- Assign responsibility fairly and correct problems that arise with group members.
- Take the blame handed out by your superiors yourself, with as few excuses as possible.

The next time someone does something wrong, point out the problem and wait. Next time you do something wrong, aim to make your apology and explanation in less than 20 words.

Women Fix Things

The urge to improve things seems to afflict many women. Problem-solving is a valuable people skill for middle managers, but beware of taking everybody's concerns and making them your own.

> Maria looked up to see Hector at her office door. "We've got a problem," he said. "I have to leave early for the next couple of days because my wife's car is in the shop, and I have to pick her up from work. I've got some overtime coming, so I can use that up, but it means I can't get the subreport done by Friday."
>
> "Can't she get a ride with someone else?" asked Maria.
>
> "Nope," said Hector.
>
> "Can you borrow someone's car, or does the shop have a loaner?"
>
> "Nope."
>
> "What about coming in earlier?"
>
> "Won't work," said Hector.
>
> "You're right," said Maria. "We have a problem."

Take a lesson from psychotherapists and help people take responsibility for solving their problems. The solutions we find for ourselves are usually more effective than those handed to us by others. Encourage and assist if necessary, but do not rush in with answers and advice every time a problem crops up. People need to take responsibility for themselves to grow.

The next time a member of your team comes to you with a problem, make a conscious effort to resist looking for solutions for them. Listen and agree that the problem exists and then ask them what they plan to do about it. Then keep quiet and wait for a reply.

Another good technique is to repeat the problem back to them to ensure you have it right and to get them focused on thinking about it some more. Then

"SHE" SAYS — "HE" SAYS

ask them their plans and wait. This is "bite your tongue" time, and you may well find it much harder to put into practice than it sounds. Like many other skills, the more you do it, the easier it becomes.

The Gender Differences That Damage Clear Communications

Men tend to display their expertise and show off skills and abilities. They want to be respected, admired and enjoy a feeling of superiority over others. Women downplay their skills and abilities and are willing to listen, support and assent when others speak, rather than simply biding their time until they can grab center stage. Even when a woman disagrees with what a man says, she will try to avoid offending him by not telling him at once, or even telling him at all.

Because women do not rush to grab the limelight or openly state disagreement, men may conclude that they are less knowledgeable, think that there is no leadership and take over.

Stating disagreement in a straightforward, unemotional way will help you get your ideas across and maintain the leadership role you have earned.

Feedback and response to conversation by women is usually constant and plentiful with verbal and nonverbal input that show complete attention.

- Men are quieter and, although they appear to be paying attention, listen less.
- Women might think that they have been heard when they have not.
- Women also pay attention to the metamessage, or what is said between the lines.
- Men do not do this as much in general.
- Women tend to get annoyed with men because they fail to read the message behind the words.
- Men challenge statements they disagree with and tend to interpret silence after a statement as agreement.

DYNAMIC COMMUNICATION SKILLS FOR WOMEN

- Women who fail to challenge or verbally disagree may find themselves labeled as inconsistent or insincere if they show disagreement later.

Say what you mean loud and clear. Do not expect men to pick up your meaning from your body language or expression. This is not a natural skill for them and they might not have learned how to do it. Make sure you have his attention before you start to speak. Men are not as adept at multitasking as women so don't pass on vital information while he is focused elsewhere.

Many women undermine their credibility by their poor choice of words. Diminutives or cute words such as "darling" to describe an object, "teeny" or "wee'est" instead of "small" and pet nicknames for co-workers might make men squirm. The problem is made worse when the woman making these inappropriate word choices is older rather than very young. But, even though some men will condone behavior from younger or more attractive women that they would otherwise condemn, they are unlikely to be so forgiving when it comes to considering people for serious promotion. A woman executive is even less likely to appreciate poor word choices since she might feel that the person speaking inappropriately demeans other women, as well as herself.

A woman might make the mistake of trying to be "one of the boys" by using a masculine style of speaking. This may be her way of coping with a male-dominated work environment, perhaps one in which there is a lot of profanity. Although our society is much less likely to outwardly condemn profanity than in the past, the fact remains that many people still dislike its usage. Older men in particular dislike its usage by women. The double standard remains alive in this area. Since those in authority in the majority of American companies are still older, white males, it might be wise to choose a better way of coping with overuse of profanity by the men in your workplace.

Always choose a style of communication that is clear and concise. Avoid any unnecessary adjectives, especially those that cloud your intent. Speaking appropriately is smart business practice. Save baby talk, endearments and pet names for your private life and delete those expletives altogether.

"She" Says — "He" Says

Competition and the importance of winning tend to make men more comfortable with acting alone and taking the initiative. Women prefer to work with others. They feel happier when consensus is reached or important decisions are shared. Men can translate this preference into a lack of decision-making by women. They might believe that women who operate this way are fearful or timid. These men might view women as too soft or vacillating for business success.

If you are uncomfortable with stating your decision in the same way men do, say so up front. Next time you are called upon to make a decision and want to consult others first, make that your decision. Say something like this, "I believe this decision is an extremely important one. I intend to run a few of the main points by some of my key people in our meeting this afternoon before I prepare my final answer. My team needs to be fully involved in all stages of this project if it is to be successful, and I value their input. I will give you my decision at 4 o'clock."

Deborah Tannen, in her book, *Women and Men in the Workplace: Language, Sex, and Power*, is careful to say that because men and women communicate differently, it is wrong to see one method as superior or inferior to the other.

These styles are apparently learned while playing in mainly same-sex groups as small children, and we cannot avoid growing up marked, to some extent, by that early experience. The difficulty seems to lie in that it is not a quickly fixed problem. Ms. Tannen notes that men tend to look for solutions when faced with problems. Women are more concerned with understanding a problem and finding ways to live with it.

She does hold out hope for a better understanding between the sexes when she writes, "As the corporate world becomes less rigidly authoritarian, and as men and women learn to become aware of one another's speaking styles, the most widely spoken language of the workplace could simply become the language of civility."

There are other glimmers of hope out there also.

- A recent study out of West Virginia University indicates that both sexes find it more comfortable to discuss serious or difficult topics in a more formal situation. This might suggest that sticking to a formal format for meetings helps everyone handle serious discussion better.

- Other studies from Washington State and Georgia universities indicate that women value and have better social support networks than do men but that neither sex finds their primary support from fellow workers. Women tend to be more sensitive when giving support, and both men and women prefer support to be provided by women. These studies seem to indicate that maintaining a more formal, less intimate style of work relationship might be beneficial to women who want to get ahead. Women need to learn to separate their work and social lives more definitively if they want to avoid being perceived as a supporter rather than a leader by others.

It's easy to fall into the trap of believing that these generalizations we have discussed in this chapter about gender differences are applicable to everyone. Of course they are not. For example, men often complain that women are too indirect, but men can be indirect when it suits them. Many men will deflect or change the topic to avoid an emotional situation that makes them feel uncomfortable.

The trick to improving your individual style is to assess yourself and work on the areas you know you have difficulty. It's also helpful to recognize where the people who give you problems are coming from and find ways to effectively cope with them. Knowledge, it has been rightly said, is power, and the aim of this book is to empower women to communicate more effectively.

As Deborah Tannen points out, this is not an impossible task. We do not need to feel intimidated or that we are incapable of finding ways to cope.

"SHE" SAYS — "HE" SAYS

> *"The sexes baffle and bewilder each other, not because they have vastly different psychological make ups, but because they have distinct conversational styles."*
> Deborah Tannen, *Are Women Too Nice in the Office?*

Eight Stereotypes Men Believe About Women's Communication Styles

1. Gossiping
2. Illogical
3. Verbose
4. Trivial
5. Emotional
6. Insecure
7. Overly polite
8. Imprecise

Reasons Behind Their Thinking

1. Men have trouble differentiating between exchanging news and malicious gossip.
2. Men's thought patterns tend to be linear, while women make more horizontal connections.
3. Women use more words than men to describe events.
4. Men tend to focus on one task or one aspect of their lives at a time. While they are so focused, other aspects become less important. Women are used to multitasking and might consider all aspects of their lives as important all the time to the extent that they do not concentrate as fully and as necessary sometimes on the task at hand.

DYNAMIC COMMUNICATION SKILLS FOR WOMEN

5. Men tend to be uncomfortable dealing with the emotions of others. Women are conditioned to be nurturing and solution-finders for others.

6. Use of questioning words and voice tones, qualifiers, reluctance to criticize and misinterpreted silences by women lead men to see them as weak, vacillating, insincere and poor leaders.

7. Men tend to expect to give and receive orders from their leaders and see politeness as a "frill" unnecessary in the main drive to get the job done. Women prefer a conciliatory, sharing, relational style with cooperative workers where the environment in which the work is done is as important as the work itself.

8. Women do in fact use more "fuzzy" words, especially adjectives, when describing an event.

What Can You Do to Avoid Being Labeled With These Stereotypes?

1. Listen but refrain from participating in gab sessions, especially during working hours.

2. Try to communicate in point fashion. Remember that men like to go from step to step and reach a conclusion. Just as you would try to help a non-English speaker understand, take this major difference in communication style into consideration when speaking to men and avoid sidetracking or jumping across points that seem unimportant or self-explanatory to you.

3. Prune your sentences. Practice this when writing and then try to carry it over into your speech. Begin by making your assignments and delegations clear and precise. Learn the value of waiting for clarification before rushing in to fill the silence.

4. Try to keep your personal life out of your business talk.

5. Choose objective words like "considerate" instead of "sweet" when thanking someone. Keep work relationships businesslike and don't offer support as a matter of course to everyone who has a problem.

"SHE" SAYS — "HE" SAYS

6. Lower your tone at the end of sentences and, when you know you are right, say your piece without asking permission, and on your own authority. Practice assertiveness skills and try some exercises to improve your self-esteem.

7. Politeness is good. Many of your foreign associates and customers will probably value it even more than the locals. As long as you are not sounding servile or begging, then stand firm on this one. It will probably serve you well in the long run.

8. It is not helpful to you or to others if your message is not understood. Men do not read between the lines very well. They do not understand what you have not said in the same way that another woman might. "Telling it like it is" is a valuable business skill, especially when dealing with co-workers of every level.

Ways to Avoid Stereotyping That DO NOT Work

1. Ignoring all gossip leaves you unpopular and uninformed.

2. Restricting yourself to totally linear thinking reduces your ability to think outside the lines and be creative in tackling problems.

3. Overrestriction will make you look sullen, dull or as if you have nothing to contribute.

4. Keeping to strictly business topics might make you sound narrow so try to read and watch informative TV programs.

5. Checking all your emotions at the door will make you look cold, disengaged or unsupportive.

6. Aggressive reaction will result in even worse labeling. Passive reaction will scuttle chances of promotion. Passive/aggressive reactions will make you look manipulative and unreliable.

7. Rudeness will result in your coming across as arrogant and overbearing.

8. Frankness needs to be handled carefully so that it does not seem tactless.

REFLECTIONS

Reflections on Gender Differences in Communication Styles

Look at the list of communication style indicators below. Underline the ones that describe your style and be honest with yourself in your assessment. Select the one that you would like to begin working on first.

Decide today to begin using the application tip or other suggestions from this book to deal with the problem.

1. Tentative when asked to make a decision

2. Questioning inflection at the end of sentences

3. Taking responsibility for the problems of others

4. Apologizing for things outside your control

5. Long-winded, unnecessary explaining

6. Adding qualifiers and intensifiers

7. Too many words

REFLECTIONS

When you have selected your starting point for communication style improvement, use the space below to write down your reasons for wanting to make the necessary changes to the way you speak. Give yourself a reasonable time frame to see a definite improvement or change take place. List any support people you may want to ask to help you in your project. Write down the first action that you will take to help you achieve your goal.

Reasons for making this change:

Time frame for change:

People who will support me:

First action I will take:

Reflections

Dynamic Communication Skills for Women

2 ASSERTIVE COMMUNICATION

> *"The assertive person can see the world from another's perspective, but not at the expense of her own needs.*
> *She recognizes the rights of other people, AND asks for what she needs."*
> Ruth Herman Siress
> *The Working Woman's Communication Survival Guide*

In the previous chapter we mentioned the need to find the assertive balance that lies between passivity and aggression. Many people think that our society is very troubled today because passivity and aggression have become pathological in many individuals. Extreme passivity results in depression and an inability to perform the simplest of actions. Extreme aggression results in violent actions, abuse and murder.

Expectations of behavior we learn as children often lead people to conclude that passivity is acceptable for women and that aggression is normal for men. Women and men who do not act in ways society deems normal are punished by ostracism or ridicule, labeling or even physical abuse.

Women in the workplace are especially vulnerable to the results of this extremely divisive and destructive system. They are victims of aggressors, derided for being aggressive themselves and yet unable to advance if they display the passivity they were expected to learn.

(A word of warning — many people are confused by and unsure of how to cope with assertive women. You will probably be labeled aggressive when you are in fact being assertive. Know yourself and refuse to take any such negative labels personally. Remember — don't take on the problems of others.)

Many people will tell you that being passive is the easy route. That is not so. Passivity leads to frustration, hidden anger and disappointment. You will feel like a doormat, used and abused, with everyone free to push you around. Extreme stress and even burnout can result from overpassivity. Some very passive people feel they are so powerless that the only way out is suicide.

Others try to fight back, but they are so distressed, the resultant outburst of aggression is ineffectual and unfocused. They quickly fall back into passivity again or act in passive/aggressive ways that are self-destructive, manipulative and unsatisfying.

Aggression seemingly works so well for some men that women might be tempted to try it. However, aggressive behavior does tend to escalate. People become bullies, always pushing their victims harder until the situation becomes violent. People who are aggressive are disliked. Others may fear them but they are not truly respected. Very aggressive women are subject to unpleasant labels, undermining of their authority and disloyalty from subordinates and peers.

Assertive behavior is harder to learn because it means changing old habits and learning new ways. It is natural to resist change, but you should attempt this one soon.

The Benefits of Assertive Behavior

- Build self-esteem
- Reduce stress
- Improve your mental health
- Improve your physical health
- Get heard
- Gain respect
- End bullying and harassment

Assertive Communication

- Stop people from taking advantage of you
- Gain control of your life
- Become promotable

A quick summation of what the alternatives imply will leave you in no doubt that choosing to become an assertive communicator is the only sensible choice to make.

- Nonassertiveness is typified by a reluctance to communicate what you really believe, think or feel.
- Aggressiveness is expression that intimidates, demeans or degrades others.
- Assertive communication is honest and displays respect for yourself as well as respect for others.

Be aware that most people will like you just fine if you are a bit of a doormat. You will always give up your turn for the other person, take the smallest cookie, volunteer to help out when someone else has a problem, take notes for the meeting and listen patiently to the office bore. You are a nice person. Men think that you are feminine, warm, motherly and a good sport. Other women like you too, and you have lots of friends at work. The problem is you don't have much respect professionally. When you need help, only the other doormats will remember all the times you went the extra mile and pitch in for you.

The decision is yours. Do you want simply to be liked or do you want some respect too? We already know that acting aggressive is not going to win friends or respect. The only way to go is to start today to learn how to communicate the assertive style that will win the respect you deserve and need if you are going to climb the ladder of career success.

- When we are passive, we let the other person do all the talking.
- When we are aggressive, we are shouting so loudly nobody else can be heard.

Only during assertive communication does true dialogue occur and a true meeting of minds take place.

It is an important part of your progress toward assertiveness in communication to remember that there are a lot of passive and aggressive people out there. Learning how to handle passivity and aggression from others will help you continue to apply assertive principles when things get difficult with your fellow workers.

Assertive communication enables you to stay in control, make choices that are beneficial to you and achieve your goals without resorting to manipulation, scheming, crushing the hopes of others or feeling powerless to reach them at all.

Assertiveness differs for individuals. Some of the suggestions in this book will be appropriate for you, and some will not. Remember who you are and don't try to change your personality — it will make you miserable to try. Assertiveness is a useful tool that you can lay aside for a while if you wish. Take it up when you need it. Apply it when you need it. Gradually, you will become accustomed to frank and forthright expressions of your thoughts, beliefs and feelings. It will become second nature to consider your needs equally with the needs of others. The more you practice assertive communication, the easier it will get.

Steps to Assertiveness

Believe that your needs are as important as the needs of others. Because assertiveness means believing that your needs are as important as the needs of others, many women will have to change the way they think before they can begin communicating more assertively.

Women tend to focus on what we don't like, stew about it until we are really upset, angry, resentful or hurt and then wonder why we can't express ourselves clearly to the person whose behavior has upset us. If the other person is a man, we come across as emotional, illogical or as having overreacted to something trivial.

Assertive Communication

A good way to start thinking about how to sound more assertive is to begin by building up your self-esteem. There are many programs, seminars, books and articles available on the benefits of becoming more self-confident. If you know your self-esteem is low, start building it up right away. There are many things you can do that will help. Here are a couple of simple suggestions for starting on the path toward giving yourself the credit that you deserve.

1. **Make a comprehensive list of all the things you do in the average day.**

    Place a star beside the things you do very well and a check beside the things you do pretty well. Focus on these things. Keep reminding yourself of them. Don't get hung up on what you can't do well.

2. **Become aware of your negative self-communication habits.**

    Listen to your inner voice. What does it say to you each day? What does it say when you make a mistake? Miss a deadline? Take criticism from someone?

    Write down some of your negative comments about yourself.

    On the opposite side of the sheet turn each one of those negatives into a positive.

Negative:	**Positive:**
I'm too stupid to learn the new program.	I can start learning a small part of the new program.

3. **Learn the "I-message" method of communication.**

    An "I-message" is just that — a message that begins with the word "I." Instead of, "You should get this done today," say, "I want this done today." Instead of, "The group suggested that we try this," say, "I suggest that we try this." Notice how powerful the "I-messages" are compared to the others.

Practice your assertive communication by learning to compose I-messages that will help you express your problems assertively, that get your needs across without demeaning others.

4. Become aware of what you really want in personal interactions.

List three or four of the problem people in your life and the things they do that bother you.

Then write down exactly what you are feeling when this behavior occurs. Jot down a suggestion or two about how you would like things to be.

Jill's boss is very abrupt and impatient. He tends to give her verbal instructions for things that he wants done in a way that sounds as if they are top priority. His brusque manner makes it difficult for Jill to ask any questions or find out when he wants things done. To accommodate his demands, Jill stops what she's doing and gets on to the new assignments. Jill often finds out afterward that the new tasks weren't as important as the work she had in progress. Here's what Jill wrote down about her boss's behavior.

Boss — He raps out orders at top speed and expects them to be followed instantly.

Feeling — His delivery style makes me nervous. I'm afraid I've missed something, even when I haven't. Sometimes I have to ditch important things I'm doing because his new order sounds urgent, and then I'm upset and left looking incompetent because my first assignment was the more important.

What I'd Like to Happen — The boss gives me orders in writing with a realistic deadline, which I can question and renegotiate if necessary.

Assertive Communication

The Assertive Message

The Assertive Template

When you (state the person's behavior in a factual, nonjudgmental way)

I feel (disclose your feelings)

Because (explain the impact on your life)

I'd prefer (describe what you want)

Here's what Jill wrote down to say to her boss:

> "When you give me orders very quickly and leave before I have a chance to ask questions, I feel worried that I may have missed something important, because I don't know what your deadline is in relation to what I'm currently working on. I'd prefer you to send me an e-mail with a priority rating. Then if I have a conflict on my schedule, I can get back to you about the matter."

Choose a time when you and your boss can meet, sit down and address your needs calmly together.

I-messages like this one avoid nonassertive traps such as blaming, emotional outbursts and failure to let the other person know what it is you really want to get across.

Six Rules for Making Effective, Assertive I-Messages

1. Be specific when describing behavior.
2. Be objective rather than impersonal.
3. Be brief; do not add qualifiers or intensifiers to the description of the behavior.
4. Be sure that you are communicating the real problem.
5. Be sure that you are communicating to the right person.

6. Be aware that you can only describe your feelings, attitudes and motives and do not make assumptions about the feelings of others.

Most people will respect and respond well to your new assertive style. Do not expect to get total agreement with your suggestions for improving things that you have prepared at the end of all your I-messages.

When composing your I-message, you will have thought of the effects the behavior has on your life. If you have to negotiate, you will need to know what the incentive is for the other person to want to change to the way you want things done in the future. Thinking about what is in it for the other person is a wise preparatory move. It will also help you to make suggestions in the "I prefer" section of the statement that are realistic and acceptable in the first place so that you will not need to negotiate.

Understand That You Have the Right to Say "No" Without Feeling Guilty

Women tend to find it hard to refuse when others ask for help. They try to be superwomen, delegating and then doing the work themselves, finding solutions to everyone's problems and taking responsibility for keeping everyone else happy.

Learning to say no when you do not have the time or the inclination to say yes is not just for others. It is your right to say no when you do not want to say yes.

Some of the benefits that go along with discovering the delights of saying no are:

- Knowing that you are not required to make excuses for or justify your decision

- Knowing that it is all right to change your mind

- Knowing that it is not the end of the world if you make a mistake

Assertive Communication

- Knowing that you do not have to have all the answers
- Knowing that you do not have to please everyone before you can deal with them
- Knowing that the way you think is just as valid as the way others think
- Knowing that you can choose to apply logic when problem-solving, or not
- Knowing that you are not obliged to care about everybody else's concerns as if they were your own
- Knowing that you are responsible for your own actions, thoughts and behaviors and that you will no longer depend upon others to validate them

Saying "No"

Use I-messages to enable others to accept that what you say is important to you and not threatening to them. This will help you to say no effectively without feeling uncomfortable.

> e.g., "I cannot help you right now. Why not ask Joe to assist you?"

or,

> "I am in the middle of supper. May I call you back in an hour?"

or,

> "I have decided not to take on that project at this time."

Learning to say no will also help you to say yes to what you want to do without getting trapped into a lot of extra add-ons or conforming to another's methods.

> e.g., "Yes, I will be able to help you complete the report, but I have only one hour available. I will have to hand back anything that is not completed by then. I'd prefer to work in my office where I can find things that I may need quickly."

As you can see, using I-messages to communicate means that you are being honest and open, while maintaining a tactful, polite and friendly manner. Most people will accept your I-messages as perfectly reasonable, valid and acceptable statements and respond accordingly.

A few, very aggressive or passive/aggressive types will not. Then, if you want to remain assertive, you will need to move to the next stage. Remember, part of being assertive is the freedom to choose to be nonassertive if you prefer. Perhaps the difficult person is someone who could become violent. Perhaps the person is an authority figure whom it would be unwise to cross. The first two assertive communication steps should not cause you problems, even if your self-confidence is still a little low. Moving ahead demands a fairly high level of self-confidence and is best tackled when you are feeling confident and empowered.

Assertion With Firmness and Confrontation

People who do not understand the meaning of "no," people with negative attitudes, or people who are unable to yield power can be hard to convince with a straightforward I-message. If you have tried that and not gotten your message across, and you want to take it further, try increasing the firmness of your statement.

Start with the basic I-message and then increase the pressure on the other person.

> e.g., Stage 1. "I need to have the monthly figures completed by noon today. I know you are busy, but I must get them in time to prepare for tomorrow's staff meeting."
>
> Stage 2. "Your schedule will have to be interrupted for today; this has priority. Make sure that you have arranged your scheduling by next month so that there are no delays in the future."
>
> Stage 3. "If you are unable to rearrange your schedule to handle the monthly figures, I will have no choice but to reassign you to a less responsible position."

Assertive Communication

Notice that the assertive statements have escalated in strength because the other person has failed to change their unacceptable behavior. Starting out at Stage 3 would have displayed aggression. Working up to Stage 3 via Stages 1 and 2 shows assertiveness, tenacity in problem-solving and a determination to have your reasonable orders followed properly.

Communication that puts increasing pressure on the one who is acting inappropriately shows leadership qualities. The problem that you had when they failed to conform to your wishes has been settled where it belongs, on the problem-maker's shoulders. Forcing the troublesome person to take responsibility for their actions and pointing out the consequences of what they do are leadership activities.

Remember, you are not responsible for others' problems. You have offered a solution that was not accepted. Now it is entirely the responsibility of the one at fault to find a reasonable solution or take the consequences.

It is perfectly acceptable to confront people who fail to keep agreements. Maintain the nonjudgmental language and matter-of-fact tone and choose objective rather than subjective words. Failing to follow through is a business no-no. Failing to call the guilty party to task will be taken as compliance, especially if that person is male.

If you fail to confront when someone has let your team down, you will not only lose the respect of the problem-maker but of your team as well. A good team leader goes to bat for her team and that might very well include confronting another team leader or even an authority figure on their behalf. A passive person who whines about the problem with the team but who will not state the problem face to face with the perpetrator will lose respect on all sides.

An effective confrontational message in this situation might be:

> "We agreed at the March meeting that my team would get a new computer to replace the one that is outdated. The decision is in the minutes, and I received and initialed your memo confirming the decision on April 3. I see that the purchase is not mentioned in the budget. I would like to ask you to revise the budget to include this item."

Avoid the Temptation to Blame

It is absolutely vital that you avoid laying blame at all stages of assertive communication. As soon as you begin blaming someone for a problem, you lay yourself open to earning a dismissive label such as whiner, shrill or emotional, especially from the men you confront.

Keep your I-messages and escalating-pressure messages free from personal comments, qualifiers and other embellishments that pull the communication down to an argument.

Just imagine the effect you would have on your supervisor if you went to bat for your team's new computer with something like this:

> "You lied! You swore we'd get a new computer and then broke your promise like it was nothing. My team is furious! It's totally devastated morale! I'll never get them working together again, not like the happy, trusting family we once were. They've been on my back since I got in, and it's all your fault. I'll never believe a word you say, ever, ever again!"

This kind of tirade will not impress any business leader, particularly if you end by getting so worked up that you yell or burst into tears of rage or both. A professional approach will get you the respect you deserve, a very good chance of a second look, or at least a reasonable explanation about the missing computer. It will certainly help you to present the image you want others to get of your potential as a leader as you progress toward your career goals.

REFLECTIONS

Reflections on Assertive Communication

Look at these inappropriate messages and try to imagine that you are receiving them rather than sending them:

1. "You're always late! It totally messes up my plans for the day."

2. "You don't appreciate anything I do for you."

3. "I've got too much to do to chat on the phone with you all day."

4. "Why do I get all the lousy jobs? You never help me when you know I'm in over my head."

In the space beneath each message, write in the feelings that you would have if someone said this to you.

An appropriate I-message, instead of the first example, might sound like: "I feel frustrated when you are late for our appointments because it throws off my schedule for the rest of the day. I prefer that we reset the meeting time to one hour later from now on. This will give you time to be on schedule."

Compose appropriate I-messages for the other three statements.

Remember to use the assertive template when composing your messages.

The words you wrote under the statements will help you to compose the first part of the I-messages.

3 IS ANYBODY LISTENING?

Four Truths About Listening

1. Listening is not a gift.
2. It is not something that others do well but that you do not have time to learn.
3. It is vital for effective management.
4. It is the area in which many executives fail to excel.

Listening is an extremely valuable skill. One of the reasons it is so valued is that it is rare. Many women believe that this is a skill that women do better than men, but this is not true. Women tend to ask too many questions that can bar effective listening.

Psychological studies rank listening as the type of support most needed by people. The numbers of people who report telling their problems to their pets further indicate that this need is very great. People even talk to themselves for lack of a good listener.

At least 40 percent of the average executive's time is spent listening. This number rises to more than 80 percent for top professionals and consultants. As you would expect from these figures, large companies recognize the need for good listening skills so that any expensive use of managerial time is not wasted. Companies spend millions each year to train their employees to listen more effectively, but most executives still have problems in this area. Learning to be a good listener, to be effective in active listening will clearly make you a valued employee and assist you as you climb the corporate ladder.

Active Listening

Effective listening involves more than simply keeping your ears open and your mouth shut, although both are important. The active listener uses the power of body language to send signals that good listening is taking place. Good listeners use body language such as forward posture and eye contact, etc. to indicate that they are paying attention.

They avoid body language that sends a metamessage of inattention. Fidgeting, looking around the room and doodling are common examples of body language that tell the other person that you are not listening.

Ask the Right Questions

A barrage of questions will discourage rather than encourage the other person to talk. Open questions that lead the person forward into explanations or deeper probing of the topic are more useful. Open questions cannot be answered by a simple yes or no.

Saying "and … " will often encourage the other person to enlarge on their topic without any need for questions. Women tend to rush into speech to cover awkward silences and make people feel more at ease. Keeping quiet or simply repeating back what the person has just said will often work better when you need more to go on before making a reply.

The advantages of keeping quiet or repeating what was said include:

- You do not rush in with a hasty, ill-judged, emotional reaction.

- You have time to make a reasoned, logical, unemotional response later, when all the facts are in.

- You do not disrupt the train of thought of the other person.

- You do not break the mood or destroy rapport.

Is Anybody Listening?

- You encourage the other person to continue giving information.

- You prevent blurting out inappropriate information to fill the conversational gap.

- You allow time to decide if you need to speak at all.

- You can help keep control of the conversation.

This ploy must be used wisely. It is not effective 100 percent of the time.

The disadvantages of failing to speak up when necessary include:

- Losing concentration and getting sidetracked into activities such as composing something clever to say rather than listening to what is being said

- Giving the impression that you have nothing to say or are in over your head

- Giving the impression that you agree with the speaker without reservation

Single syllable words such as "and" or "yes" along with nods and shaking your head will help others know that you are indeed listening. An interested facial expression that lets the other person know you are sympathetic to what is being expressed is also helpful. The reason why many men have problems conveying their listening ability is because they have been accustomed to doing business with a poker face.

Daniel Coleman, in his book, *Working With Emotional Intelligence*, tells us that one of the highly valued traits that most top professionals possess is empathy. Empathy lets the other person know that their concerns are being heard and understood. A nonjudgmental, open and empathetic atmosphere is vital for good listening. The average speaker will clam up if they feel belittled, disbelieved or undervalued by the listener. Persons who interrupt or who send inappropriate, nonempathic or impatient metamessages make poor listeners. Such people do not make good managers. They tend to skip the first step of problem-solving, which is to listen and completely understand the problem.

Dynamic Communication Skills for Women

This results in incomplete or ineffective resolutions, staff who are reluctant to express concerns, and negative attitudes in the workplace.

Women's Intuition

Reading body language, sensing the atmosphere and interpreting the metamessages of others are skills that many women possess. They rely on and value their intuitive abilities when they make decisions and judge others. Men do this too. Daniel Coleman tells us that gut feelings and first impressions are widely used by the most successful people, men as well as women, to help them in their business endeavors.

It is better probably for women, who know the value of their intuition, to simply adopt the more masculine terminology and switch to gut reaction or feeling when describing their feelings, rather than the women's intuition term that many men find hard to take. They should also be aware that men do not look for metamessages, or unspoken messages, to understand what the other person really means, especially when talking with men. Use clear, unambiguous I-messages and You-messages to get your views heard rather than relying on the other person to pick up your unspoken thoughts.

Concentrate on Them

The big problem for listeners is transferring full attention to the speaker, totally. This is hard to do. The more important your position and the more others defer to your opinion, the harder it becomes to listen to the opinions of others attentively.

Because women tend to consider the feelings, needs and status of others ahead of their own, they can often do this better than men. When women learn how to become assertive, they must retain the ability to focus on the other person so that they will continue to show effective, active listening skills. Aggressive people are extremely poor listeners. Concentrating on the other person is the first and most important step toward convincing that person to open up to you.

Is Anybody Listening?

First You Must Get Their Attention!

We often fail to get others to listen to us because we fail to get their full attention in the first place. If you know you need to take time and get together for a serious talk, set up an appointment. It is hard to give the serious attention that serious problems deserve when you are distracted by noise and interruptions, conscious of some other pressing engagements or concentrating on other matters.

Asking for or giving quality time so that clear communication can take place pays off and will actually save time later. Putting off difficult people who you do not want to deal with is a waste of time too. Take time and listen, so that you can come to a satisfactory, final conclusion. Letting the other person feel fairly treated and making a proper decision is the professional way to handle those awkward cases. It will also get the problem handled in the shortest time. Putting people off, playing telephone tag or promising to meet and postponing will take up far more of your valuable time in the long run.

Why Good Listening Does Not Happen

- People are approached when they are distracted by other activities.

    e.g., Someone grabs at your sleeve in the hall as you are heading to a meeting and wants to talk about redecorating the coffee room.

- People are given important messages at inappropriate times.

    e.g., The supervisor is down on the shop floor looking at the new punch press robot, and the foreman is trying to explain that the skylight in the tool room is leaking.

- Vital information is tossed out in the middle of a lot of other less important talk.

    e.g., The chief accountant murmurs, "And the sales figures for June seem rather odd," in the middle of a list of figures during his usual half-hour report on the budget at the monthly executive meeting.

- The information is unclear or very technical, and you are too hurried or too unwilling to look foolish to ask for clarification.

    e.g., The chief engineer has just run over the new computer program he has put together. You understood one word in 10, but he sneers when people ask him for clarification, so you nod and say you think it's great just to get rid of him. Later, you discover that the new program vitally affects the productivity of your department.

- The speaker has a speech or mannerism problem.

    e.g., James is your supervisor. The other people in the office giggle about his pompous mannerism and imitate him behind his back because he rocks back and forth on his heels and rises slowly up on his toes as he talks. You spend all the time while he is talking to you at your desk trying not to laugh.

- The speaker is, or reminds you of, someone you have had problems with in the past.

    e.g., Your boss looks very much like a teacher who was very tough on you in school. She screamed at you and hit your hands with a ruler. Your boss isn't likely to yell at you much less hit you, but you can't stop feeling nervous when you have to go to her office. You get so tense that you can't concentrate on what she is saying no matter how hard you try.

Five Attention-Getters That Encourage Active Listening

1. Saying the listener's name aloud at the beginning of the opening sentence

    e.g., "Rachel, the figures you wanted are complete."

2. A joke, quote or anecdote that is relevant to the person or topic

    e.g., "I was talking to the chief of Herriot Brothers yesterday, and he asked me who our most innovative design person was, so of course I told him about you."

Is Anybody Listening?

3. An object, picture or handout of some kind that is relevant to the person or topic

   e.g., "Look at this old photograph of them beginning to build our plant. We should start thinking about marking our 50th anniversary in some way, don't you think?"

4. A startling question or exaggerated statement relevant to the person or topic

   e.g., "Have you ever killed anyone? Well, you will be answering yes if we don't do something about this guardrail replacement."

5. Letting the other person know first what's in it for them

   e.g., "You will save an average of $2,000 per shift if you bite the bullet and make the line changes I suggested in the last report."

Increase your listening skills if you want to become an excellent communicator.

REFLECTIONS

Reflections on Effective Listening Skills

The next time you have the opportunity, try this experiment/exercise. *Warning, do not attempt this during an important discussion. Choose an occasion when you are with friends or in some informal setting.

While someone is talking to you, deliberately use body language and expressions that indicate you are not listening.

Try things like:
- Losing eye contact
- Yawning or looking bored
- Humming
- Fiddling with your hair or nails
- Doodling
- Looking at someone else or listening in on another conversation

Keep this up for a couple of minutes and observe what happens to the speaker. This person will probably:
- Start losing track of words being spoken
- Lean closer to you or grab your arm
- Talk louder
- Get annoyed

So don't keep it up too long.

REFLECTIONS

Apologize for being inattentive and begin using body language and expressions that indicate you are listening.

Try things like:
- Keeping eye contact
- Nodding and shaking your head in response
- Saying "yes," "no" or "and" to encourage them to continue

Notice how much more comfortable the speaker is and how readily he or she continues talking when it can be seen that you are listening.

Reflections

4 NONVERBALS: THE UNSPOKEN LANGUAGE OF COMMUNICATION

We are accustomed to reading unspoken messages when we communicate with others. The skill of understanding and sending nonverbal messages is found in small children and also in many animals. Attitudes, body posture, gestures, facial expressions and sounds make up a huge vocabulary that expresses our thoughts, feelings and understanding to others, more clearly than words.

Research indicates that most people tend to believe the unspoken message before the spoken one. This means that if your body language or facial expression is incongruent or does not match what you are saying, then the listener will believe not what is being said but what they think your nonverbal signs are telling them.

Body language in most social animals, such as wolves or deer, shows that the subservient animals understand who is leader and defer properly. The leader's posture and actions indicate dominance.

Humans are social animals too. It is interesting that we also recognize leaders and defer to them through body language. Our modern Western society is less hierarchical and structured, so we tend to get our signals mixed up sometimes. However, most people still notice and respond to dominating body language.

Leaders are wise if they learn to use body language to increase their assertiveness. Dominating others is not usually necessary, although it might be useful to know how to do so in dealings with difficult people. It is possible to look assertive and powerful without crushing others with oppressive body language. Learning to make yourself look more in control, more decisive and more like a leader, however, is smart business practice for those who want to get ahead.

Believe It First

Just acting assertive is not going to convince people that you are assertive. The most important thing to learn about acting out a principle that you don't believe in your heart, is that it will not convince others. However, acting as if you are convinced will help you become convinced. Then, when you have convinced yourself, you also will convince others.

Just remember the old song that says, "I whistle a happy tune, whenever I feel afraid." The song goes on to say that the act of whistling and sounding unconcerned eventually makes the person really be unafraid. Some people call this "fake it 'till you make it."

Observing how good leaders act will give you excellent pointers for making your behavior more convincing. This is one reason why a wise choice of a mentor is so useful when you are starting to climb the corporate ladder. A strong leader, one you truly admire, will give you a pattern to follow. You should notice the posture, gestures, expressions and habits of your mentor and try to incorporate those that seem effective into your dealings with others. Having a good female mentor helps a woman learn effective, feminine nonverbal skills. Sometimes women with good male mentors take on male body language that is confusing or uncomfortable both for themselves and for others. Choose nonverbals with which you are comfortable. Otherwise, you will continue to look phony, no matter how hard you try to make them work for you.

Some nonverbals are hard to control. Reactions to a person who rubs you the wrong way or who reminds you of someone you dislike are very hard to keep neutral.

NONVERBALS: THE UNSPOKEN LANGUAGE OF COMMUNICATION

The Way We Communicate

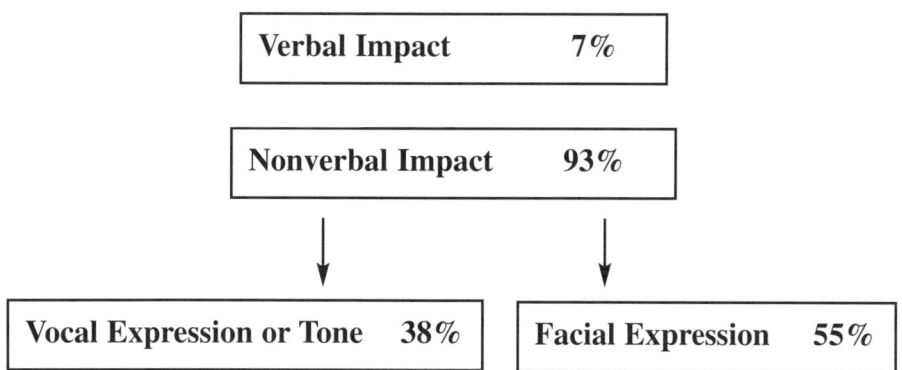

Types of Nonverbal Communication

Poker Face

Male leaders often like to keep a poker face. They express less emotion and smile less often and less broadly than others. This impassive behavior indicates that one does not have to be pleasing to others. Women tend to smile and use a wider variety of facial expressions. If you are comfortable with calming down your facial responses, you will probably come across as more powerful to others, and they may even try to please you by their reactions to you when you speak. Beware of looking cold or uninterested. Remember, women are expected to be warmer than men in dealing with others. However, it is a fact that while a hearty laugh, when appropriate, will not lower your power rating, smiling all the time for no reason can make you look foolish.

Masterful Tone

Many people, both men and women, equate power and authority with a deep, masculine voice. Of course, as a woman you do not want to adopt a bass voice, but it is not such a bad thing to consider how your present tone affects your audience.

Dynamic Communication Skills for Women

Assertive, dynamic voices are:

- Firm
- Strong
- Self-confident
- Relaxed
- Varied — loud when necessary, quiet when getting attention, get the other person to focus on them
- Low-pitched — especially at the ends of sentences
- Well-modulated

Unassertive voices sound:

- Whiny
- Tentative
- Questioning
- Weak and inaudible
- Dying away before finishing a sentence
- Prissy
- Nagging
- Snappy or petty
- Hectoring or schoolmarmish

Many women have voices which do not lower much in tone as they become mature women. They continue to sound girlish. These women often have trouble gaining credibility in business. They might have trouble getting people to believe them on the telephone or when giving instructions to subordinates.

NONVERBALS: THE UNSPOKEN LANGUAGE OF COMMUNICATION

After she became the Queen of England, Elizabeth II had to take elocution lessons to change her girlish voice and lower her voice pitch a few notches.

Listen to yourself on voice mail or take a tape recorder to the office for the day. You will be surprised how different you sound to others. When we hear our voices, the bones of our skull distort the sound and make it different from the way others hear us. The recording will give you a truer impression of how others hear you.

If you decide to make some changes to your tone, practice alone before trying it on others. Remember that this is a "fake it 'till you make it" ploy. Record yourself as you practice speaking in a lower pitched voice and then listen for unassertive sounds that others might be picking up on when you speak.

A well-modulated, overly expressive voice might actually be less assertive than a flatter, less expressive delivery. High status males tend to use less voice expression to match their poker faces. Take a tip from them and don't overdo the expressiveness unless you have the sort of job, such as public speaking or teaching, that demands it.

Look 'Em Square in the Eye

Many people think that the eyes are the most important feature for reading nonverbal communication. They search the other person's eyes for clues to what they are thinking and feeling. These people notice when a smile is not reflected in the other person's eyes or when they fail to make eye contact at all. Many people regard that failure as indicative of dishonesty or an uneasy conscience.

Some cultures have problems with eye contact. They find it invasive or rude. These cultural differences can give rise to misunderstandings in communication. A lot, but not all, of body language is universal. Being aware of cultural differences is the sign of an alert, considerate person who is astute when dealing with others.

People with poor self-esteem often display low confidence by failing to make eye contact. They do not want to draw attention to themselves, and just like children in school who do not know the answer, they believe that if they do not look at the other party, they will be unnoticed.

Lengthy or intense eye contact can be interpreted in other ways. Some people seek to dominate by holding eye contact for a long time in an effort to make the other person blink first. This habit stems from childish games, but some people continue to practice it in later life, much to the discomfort of those they deal with. Glaring or lengthy eye contact also expresses anger, impatience or a desire to challenge. Staring or lengthy eye contact might suggest sexual attraction and could be construed as harassing behavior.

Most of us tend to look at, and make eye contact with, those we feel are our friends, supporters or who give us approval.

Give Me Some Space

We are territorial creatures. When someone else invades our personal space, we feel uncomfortable and offended.

Dominant people tend to call subordinates into their territory so that they have the home ground advantage. The higher the workplace status, the bigger and often, quite literally, the higher from the ground their territory gets. People tend to protect their territory from others and resent their intrusions. Even when the only territory we have is our personal space, we are still resentful of the intrusions others make into it.

Special elevators, imposing furniture, high, long hallways, outer offices, secretaries and personal assistants, acres of expensive carpeting and huge imposing desks guard the extended territory of the top executive from invasion.

The average woman starting out in business has only her assertive body language to keep her personal space from being invaded by those seeking to dominate her and keep her submissive.

Dominance-seeking invasions of your space include:

- Standing too close
- Looming over you so that you are forced to look up or move back

NONVERBALS: THE UNSPOKEN LANGUAGE OF COMMUNICATION

- Sitting on your desk
- Standing up while you are forced to remain seated
- Placing themselves with their backs to the light
- Picking up and inspecting personal items on your desk
- Dropping by your office frequently without being invited
- Sitting down in your office without being invited
- Touching you in any way that makes you feel uncomfortable
- Maneuvering you into a corner
- Doing anything to you that you do not feel is permissible to do to them

Take back your territory by:

- Making an I-statement that tells how you feel and what you prefer
- Moving away
- Having loomers sit down
- Moving around your office as you talk
- Indicating the chair you want the visitor to take
- Stop speaking about the topic at hand and explaining all the items on your desk in a calm expressionless way to the casual picker-upper, before continuing with your business discussion
- Telling casual droppers-by that you are busy right now, but that they can call you later if they need to speak to you about something
- Continuing to work and not appearing to notice them
- Getting up and indicating that you have another meeting or have to see someone else

- Placing yourself on the same status level as the dropper-by — drop by on them yourself

- Shutting your door or creating some other barrier to let people know when visitors are not welcome

Touching or any other behavior that is harassing may be reported as harassment if it makes you uncomfortable. Warning the offender that you will do this might be all that is necessary. Harassers who do not heed warnings must be stopped. Always follow through on warnings that you give. Do not give warnings that you are unable or unwilling to follow up on.

I Don't Get Any Respect Around Here

Status symbols, office precedence, addressing by title, keys to the executive restroom, access to the director's lounge, executive travel arrangements and a marked parking space near the door are just a few of the special communicators of personal prestige that top executives struggle to achieve and resent losing. Getting and keeping the outward signs of status drive many people to keep on climbing the ladder of success.

You will probably want to have others recognize and give you the respect you know you deserve. How you do this depends on your own determination. Having others address you by your title used to be a good way of communicating status. Today, we are less formal at work. Many top executives feel that it makes them appear more modern and forward-looking if they allow everyone to address them by their first names. If you start insisting on a title in that kind of situation, you will look old-fashioned or overly formal.

Ignoring status symbols or the privileges of rank that others in your company clearly expect and enjoy can make it look as if you are uncaring of success or not one of the group when it comes to seeking out higher management material.

I Hate Those Limp Handshakes

It has been traditionally acceptable for hundreds of years for men to shake hands when meeting and parting. The right hand is used to indicate that no weapon is being concealed and that the approach is friendly. Traditionally,

NONVERBALS: THE UNSPOKEN LANGUAGE OF COMMUNICATION

women have not been involved in shaking hands. More recently, women have shaken hands socially only selectively.

Business handshakes are part of making a good first impression. They establish that contact has been made, introductions have been heard and that networking can commence. The handshake will show intent to deal and even provide acknowledgment that a deal has been made. The handshake is as binding as a written contract in many cultures and is tantamount to giving a verbal promise in others.

Women in business should shake hands as freely and with the same intent as men. A firm, dry, warm, handshake is often taken as a positive indicator when getting that all-important first impression. This impression applies to men and women alike. Beware, though, of the man who attempts to intimidate you by too firm a grip.

A loose, very brief handshake indicates a lack of involvement or interest in the other party. You may feel reluctant to shake hands with people you dislike. Refusing to shake hands indicates strong dislike, snubbing or distrust. It is always considered an insult, like slamming the door in the face of, hanging up on, or refusing to speak to the offended party.

Assertive handshakes are fairly brief, warm and firm. They will give you a professional appearance, especially if accompanied by a smile and the repetition of the person's name. Some older men still wait for the woman to initiate the handshake, so do not hesitate to do so, even if the other person has a higher status and should initiate. His reticence is probably due to the social manners he learned in his youth when women always initiated contact when being introduced.

Limp, cold handshakes are repugnant to almost everybody. They make the person seem cold, detached, unfriendly or unwell.

The Right Suit Won't Get You in the Board Room, but the Wrong One Will Keep You Out

We only have 7-13 seconds to make that all-important first impression. How you look is obviously important to making the impression you want to make.

Some companies or professions have an established dress code or require that a uniform be worn. If that is the case, then personal grooming each day and wearing the right thing to any social functions that you must attend are all you need to worry about. Most people have to choose what to wear daily and select something appropriate for casual days too.

The way you dress shows more than just fashion sense. It can also indicate your self-confidence, how much you care about fitting in with the group, or even your competence in making good choices and decisions. Dressing appropriately is the key.

It is always safer to be more conservative in your choice of what to wear at work, unless you are in an industry that values individuality or flamboyance. Once again, it may help to have a mentor or role model you admire to show you the way.

Dress choice sends messages to others about how you see yourself. Remember that people will often take your word for it when you send them messages about yourself, and nonverbal messages are even stronger than words.

Dressing well on a limited budget is not easy. Choose a store where you feel at home and get to know someone on staff who will give you honest answers when you are shopping for work wear. Shop with a friend you know will give you good advice.

Clothes that feel comfortable are best for work. There is enough stress in your day without worrying if your skirt is too tight. Keep clothes in good repair so that hems do not come down or buttons fall off just before an important presentation. Use lots of napkins at lunch and avoid messy foods during the day. Clean off stains and keep laundry up to date so that you don't get caught facing a trip out of town with nothing to wear.

NONVERBALS: THE UNSPOKEN LANGUAGE OF COMMUNICATION

The way your shoes fit actually shows up on your face. Stress and discomfort from poorly fitting shoes will affect everything you do and say. Most of us have enough trouble staying positive without the burden of painful feet to add to our struggles.

When you have climbed to the top of the corporate ladder, you can relax and wear whatever you like. The CEO wanders in wearing his golf shirt, and nobody turns a hair. Until then, dress for success by noticing what the accepted norm is and complying with that to the best of your ability.

Stand Up for Yourself

Your body language sends signals that indicate your attitude through the way you stand and move around. Others will label you "aggressive," "passive" or "assertive" according to your posture and the way you move.

> *"In our culture relaxation-tension is a very important way in which status differences are subtly conveyed."*
> Mehrabrian

Research shows that, in the Western world, men take up more relaxed poses than women. They do this whether they are with other men or with women. You have probably noticed how often men sit back in their chairs with their hands linked behind their heads and elbows out. This is communicating territorial ownership. They may lodge an ankle over the opposite knee or put their feet up on the desk until they are almost sprawling. They will wedge the telephone receiver against their shoulder and chat away for long periods, seemingly totally at ease.

Women almost never do anything like this, especially when others are present, and most especially at work.

Posture, like all communication media, is read and understood and then responded to subconsciously. Remember that men usually respond to passivity or silence as assent or agreement. Male posture or movement that attempts to intimidate by appearing overly or inappropriately casual demands a response from you if you want to stay assertive.

Just because males are not necessarily looking deliberately for signs of weakness does not mean that they will not instinctively take advantage of the weakness they observe.

Men may sprawl out and act very relaxed in your office in an attempt to indicate that they have control of the territory. Most male peers will respond by acting in the same way in the other person's territory to establish equality or at least negate the other's claim to superiority. If you are comfortable with this, then responding in the same way will send the same message for you as it does for another man.

You will probably not want to sprawl around, although leaning back and stretching out your legs in front of you with one arm resting on the chair arm and the other on your lap makes a more feminine alternative that gives a relaxed appearance with assertive signals attached. Walking around the office and examining personal photographs, etc., is another ploy men use to take control of a space and returning the behavior will once again restore balance.

If you are not at ease with reciprocal actions to strike a balance of power or if the offender is of higher status and is abusing his power, then use the assertive I-message to express your feelings and preferences as discussed in the previous chapter.

Take a Stand

The most effective way to handle the whole business of posture and body movement is to take the initiative. Avoid having to respond by looking assertive yourself. People are much less likely to try intimidating body postures if you look like the assertive person you are.

John Malloy, author of *Women's Dress for Success*, has done some interesting research into male posture and body language. He discovered that posture denotes status in males. Women can learn to read male status and take advantage of the knowledge by copying some appropriate male postures themselves.

NONVERBALS: THE UNSPOKEN LANGUAGE OF COMMUNICATION

- Higher status males tend to stand with the head and neck erect. Lower status men stoop forward and keep their chins tucked in.

- Standing still, feet slightly apart, head and neck straight, and with the hands cupped at the sides is a powerful stance. When women adopt this stance, it will send out the same message for them as it does for men.

- The powerful person will also walk differently. A straight and upright stance with even strides of about 12 inches, looking ahead with the arms at the sides and hands cupped as when standing. This pose may suggest a military bearing, but it is in fact relaxed, with smooth, unhurried movements. The higher status person looks at ease and yet ready to spring into action at any time.

- Less powerful people show tension or unevenness of stride. They slouch and look down. They sway their bodies and swing their arms more than higher status individuals.

Practice some of these tips from John Malloy's research findings for yourself. Malls and large stores often have mirrors that you can use to check your walk. Shop windows will reflect you enough to see your posture.

Begin practicing the stance and walk that will send others the signals that say this is a strong, dynamic individual. Walking like a leader won't make you a leader tomorrow, but it will help others, including those in authority, to see you as such a person. Remember, you need to think of yourself as a leader as you practice your power pose to make it a natural part of the real you. People believe your body language if you believe it first.

Being Tall Really Does Give an Unfair Advantage

Tall people do get more respect in business. Not only that, but tall, good-looking, slender people get more chances when it comes to promotion, pay increases and recognition.

Women are on average about four to five inches shorter than men, a difference that can translate into a difference of up to $3,000 in additional pay!

Not only are most men taller than most women, they try to intimidate women by looming over them, standing while a woman is seated or standing too close.

Think Big

It is possible to convey a taller image through the body language you use.

Dress Up: Color choice, construction lines, patterns, fabrics and styles can create the illusion that you are taller. Get help from the experts here. Find a manufacturer of business clothing that you know makes clothes that compliment your style and stick with them. This will prevent you making costly mistakes, buying impulsively, or forgetting what works best to give you the image you want. Usually, dark, one-color, narrow, vertical stripes, small patterns, flowing, unbroken lines and minimal accessories will help you look taller, slimmer, and more businesslike as well.

Walk Up: Imagine that your spinal cord is a rope. Every time you stand up, be conscious of straightening the rope and assuming an erect, head-up, chin-up and neck-elongated stance before you begin to move. Imagine an unseen hand is pulling the rope up through the top of your head toward the ceiling. After a while, it will become second nature to do this brief exercise.

Think Up: Your first reaction when others try to physically intimidate you by postures that stereotype you as small, short, inferior or low status should be to start thinking of yourself as the person you want to be. Think of yourself as tall, assertive, high status and the proper size for the dynamic, powerful kind of person you are.

You will probably find that thinking about yourself positively will negate the other's attempt to belittle you right away.

NONVERBALS: THE UNSPOKEN LANGUAGE OF COMMUNICATION

Here are some quick tips to combat commonly used nonverbal aggression.

If a Man Does This:	Do:	Don't:
Looms over you while you are sitting down	Casually move back and stand up if he will not sit down when you ask.	Stay sitting and look up at him.
Touches you while explaining, talking or walking along	Move away. Fold your arms. Tell him he is invading your personal space.	Smile and look down. Smooth your hair or your clothing.
Sprawls in an exaggeratedly relaxed posture in your space	Assume a relaxed posture. Move around freely in his space as soon after as possible.	Assume a closed posture. Lose eye contact.

Assertive Body Language Most Often Used by Higher Status Business People

- Looking forward, head up, relaxed walk with straight, erect posture
- Expansive, relaxed, open gestures
- Standing tall
- An open, friendly expression
- Eye contact when speaking or listening to an individual
- Freedom to turn away from people or move around while talking with a group
- Asymmetrical placement of arms and hands
- Leaning back in a chair
- Moderate-sized smiles and appropriately timed, hearty laughter

Effective managers prefer to use body language that indicates control coupled with approachability. Managers who are tense, wary, nervous, overvigilant or unsmiling are intimidating to workers of inferior status and are less effective. Moving quietly or quickly or using small, closed gestures indicates meanness and sneakiness and results in a lack of trust. Being overly effusive and noisy or joking around too much and patting people on the back or hugging makes others uneasy. This behavior will result in a loss of respect and ineffective leadership.

REFLECTIONS

Reflections on Actions That Speak Louder Than Words

Circle passive, nonverbal activities from the column on the left that you feel are hampering you in your drive to achieve leadership status.

Underline nonverbal activities from the column on the right that you will begin to adopt as you seek to become more dynamic.

Passive Nonverbals	**Assertive Nonverbals**
Fiddling with objects or accessories	Loosely clasped or steepled hands
Patting hair or touching self	Keeping hands still
Smoothing skirt or other clothing	Arms in a relaxed, asymmetric pose
Arms folded tight across chest	Holding hands and arms by your sides
Head tilted	Head straight
Looking down	Making eye contact
Brief, limp handshake	Firm, friendly handshake
Hesitant handshake	Initiates handshake
Watchful, turning to keep others in view	Casual, moving around, free to turn away
Slumped, stooping posture	Standing straight
Looking up at others	Moving back to get level eye contact
Gestures that do not match words	Coherent gestures
High-pitched tone of voice	Low-pitched tone, especially at sentence end
Weak, soft voice	Speaks up
Monotonous, whiny voice	Sounds assertive when speaking
Yells to gain attention	Speaks softly to gain attention
Cannot get attention	Uses verbal skills to gain attention
Stands with weight on one leg	Stands with feet apart, weight evenly spread

Remember:
1. You must believe in yourself before others will believe in you.
2. What you truly believe about yourself will be what others believe about you.
3. Practice the nonverbal assertive behaviors that you want to use to present a more dynamic image so that they will become real for you and allow others to get the impression of you that you want.

5 HANDLING THE BIG FOUR — CONFLICT, CRISIS, CRITICISM AND COMPLIMENTS

Conflict

We humans are social creatures, but it seems that we are unable to socialize for very long without coming into conflict with one another. This is as true in our working relationships as it is in our private lives. Misunderstandings, mistakes and misapprehensions are behind most conflicts.

Conflict might be a symptom of hidden problems, unresolved dissent or an unstated desire to dominate. Conflict might cause fresh problems, more dissent and future power struggles. Conflict is bound to occur when individuals are thrown together for long periods, such as in the workplace.

Many supervisors and managers make the mistake of imposing settlements, refusing to allow dissent, ignoring personal clashes or otherwise pretending that conflict does not happen in their departments. Studies conducted to investigate family conflict show that this method of handling problems is not helpful. The ability to engage in argument, with open expression of disagreement, is actually less harmful to individual feelings of self-worth as well as long-term relationships.

Applying this principle at work is difficult. Disruptions because of conflict are time-consuming. They affect productivity, efficiency and might even spill over into customer relations, employee downtime and company structure. However, a disruption while conflict is unresolved is better than a phony, imposed peace waiting to explode into destructive negativity.

Dr. Cherie Carter-Scott, in her book *Negaholics No More*, gives many examples of how destructive behavior arises out of unresolved problems from the past. Lowered self-esteem seems to be the outcome for many people who are not allowed to voice dissent or who find their power and control constantly threatened by others.

Conflict, if it is handled well, can provide stimulus for new ideas and creativity.

Destructive conflict involves personal attacks, name-calling, sabotage, backstabbing or even physical violence. This behavior is far from a healthy venting of views, disagreements or everyday competitive spirit between teams and team members.

Learning to handle conflict before it results in negative behavior or attitudes is the task of the effective leader. Knowing when to step in to assist people toward win-win solutions or other reasonable resolutions of conflict is a skill you can learn.

Recognize the Combatants

Strangely enough, groups or teams work together better when they are composed of varied, rather than similar personality types. Recognizing these types will help you know the best way to approach them at all times. When the going gets rough, this knowledge will be especially valuable. People handle conflict differently.

1. **The Avoider**

    This type of person will bend over backward to keep things going smoothly. They hate and fear conflict and will do anything to avoid it. Men and women can be Avoiders, but they more often are women. Forcing these people to face and express conflicting points of view will be difficult. The problem is that they might appear peaceful but are seething inside. Repressed anger and resentment is always disruptive when it finally breaks out. Avoiders have low self-esteem and might become workers with a negative attitude.

HANDLING THE BIG FOUR

2. **The Accommodator**

   Like the Avoider, the Accommodator is also more likely to be a woman than a man. She feels responsible for making everyone happy. Not only is there no room for conflict in the Accommodator's world, but there is no room for unhappiness either. She is the kind of woman who apologizes to everyone when it rains at the company picnic. She wants harmony at any price and feels responsible for making the workplace harmonious. This can result in a loss of contact with reality, denial that problems exist and even hiding problems to make the dream world come true.

   Accommodating is fine when there are minor upheavals that do not matter much to anyone. If you are more concerned with keeping relations sweet than resolving a problem, then it will work just fine to keep things calm while tempers cool.

   Accommodation is a temporary solution only.

3. **The Competitor**

   More men than women tend to be strongly competitive, although this gender distinction seems to be blurring a little in our modern world. Competitors are often helpful in business. They spur others on to make greater efforts, drive inventiveness and motivate others as well as themselves. The problems arise when Competitors are not able to let others win at any price. These people are power freaks who will never accept a win-win solution or agree to disagree. They have strongly expressed opinions, always think that they are right, and lack respect for the feelings and opinions of others. They might become aggressive, abusive or even violent in their need to maintain control of every situation.

   A competitive approach works when everyone is willing to accept the power position of the resolver or when there is an emergency demanding quick, decisive answers.

This type of resolution will always result in conflict later. Like gunfighters in the Old West, competitors seem to invite the competition they constantly strive to overcome.

4. **The Compromiser**

   Not only do the Compromisers want everyone to get along, but they also want to be fair. Principles of justice and democracy are important to the Compromiser, who wants everyone to play by the rules. Finding an acceptable compromise can indeed be a way of resolving some conflicts, especially if everyone involved agrees on what the rules are. This person can become rigid and authoritarian. They might sound judgmental or pedantic to others. The compromises they impose might not actually satisfy any dissenting parties or handle the underlying cause of a conflict.

   Compromise works best when there is no time to spare for lengthy negotiations, and both sides will get some benefit from the imposed resolution.

   This is not a perfect method because everyone loses something too, and the solution is not personally evolved but imposed from outside.

5. **The Negotiator**

   Negotiators work to find acceptable solutions to conflict. Negotiators, who have learned how to use good negotiating methods and techniques, are a great asset in any group. Supervisors or team leaders who are skilled at negotiation will probably be the best at handling conflict.

   Negotiating is the best technique for getting win-win solutions, but it relies on all parties being willing to negotiate to succeed fully. It also takes time and might be difficult to do if there is an emergency or if sufficient time is unavailable.

HANDLING THE BIG FOUR

If you feel that one of the first four personality types best describes the way you handle conflict, begin today to learn more about negotiation. Negotiating skills can be learned by anyone who is willing to try. Using negotiating techniques to settle conflicts in your department will enhance your ability as a leader.

Knowing which style of dealing with conflict works best in individual situations is a valuable leadership ability. No one method works best in all situations, and a strong leader will assess the conflict situation by various methods to know which resolution to use for the best result in each specific case.

Talking is often the cause of conflict, but it is also the means of resolution.

The first step in getting a resolution is getting people to talk.

Women in Conflict

Some women tend to plunge into conflict and conflict resolution without regard for timing or the personalities involved. This often results in an escalation of the conflict. Hasty words, inappropriate expressions and highly charged emotions that cloud issues, pull innocent bystanders into the dispute, and exacerbate the situation are almost always a result of this timing problem. Resolving fiercely emotional conflicts needs to be done in stages to allow for firm, lasting and acceptable resolutions to be found and put in place.

The first goal of conflict resolution then, especially for women, is to lower the emotional temperature by deliberately taking these three steps:

1. Treat all parties with respect.

2. Listen and try to empathize with all sides.

3. Allow all parties to state their views, feelings, needs and preferences.

A cooling-off period might have to be imposed and a time set for proper negotiations later when things have calmed down. Settling how and when these negotiations will take place and agreeing on who will be involved is a sensible step. Some conflicts need external arbitration or the input of a disinterested third party. Setting the scene for sensible resolution creates an atmosphere conducive to settlement and raises expectations that the conflict will be resolved.

Sweeping problems under the rug or avoiding issues will only cause future conflict or resentment because the problem was not addressed. A cooling-off period allows time to define and understand the root of the conflict, discover what is open to negotiation and what is not, and work with combatants individually, if necessary, before deciding on the best course of action in getting a resolution. Using good listening skills, asking open-ended questions, repeating statements and waiting for elaboration are all good techniques for getting to the truth.

Hasty judgments of who is right or wrong will not resolve the problem nor should you simply adopt the view of the majority of the onlookers as to who is at fault. Good, clear, unbiased information will help you facilitate a good, clear, unbiased resolution.

Learn From the Experience

Whether you are using these techniques to handle your conflicts better or to help you resolve conflicts between other workers, you need to recognize that they can provide you with valuable experience and opportunities to learn and grow. Evaluation after the conflict has been resolved will prepare you for dealing with the next one even more effectively.

Ask yourself:

- What have I learned about my personal conflict-resolution style?
- What have I learned about the individuals involved in this conflict?
- Have I suffered personally because of this conflict?

HANDLING THE BIG FOUR

- How can I help myself heal and become stronger?
- How badly were others hurt in this conflict?
- What can I do to help my workers heal, learn and grow?
- What can I do to prevent similar conflicts?
- Was there any profit from this conflict?
- Has any change happened — good or bad — following this conflict?
- What would I do differently next time?

Are You Part of the Problem or Part of the Answer?

Your assessment process might lead you to conclude that you are involved in conflicts more often than is reasonable or necessary. You might be combative by nature or perhaps competitive. Aggressive behavior is not helpful if you want to move ahead in today's corporate world. Assertive behavior is what you are striving to develop to help you reach the higher status you want.

Extreme behavior usually stems from deeply rooted causes that simple conflict resolution (on a workplace level) cannot hope to address. Be aware that such behavior as anger, resentment, revenge, overwhelming emotional outbursts and physical violence will not vanish unaided. Far from giving you the power and control you crave, they will prove self-destructive if unchallenged.

Most modern companies are all too aware of the problems caused by violence in the workplace. They are wary of being held liable for the actions of abusive employees. Superiors who yell or swear at workers are not suffered in silence as they may have been in the past. You will not be considered as a good candidate for promotion, even if you drive your team to high productivity and efficiency levels in the short term, if you are an abusive manager. Similarly, quarrels with peers will not earn you the respect and support that are necessary for advancement. It is true that what goes around comes around. We do indeed reap what we sow.

DYNAMIC COMMUNICATION SKILLS FOR WOMEN

Using assertive behavior and restricting confrontation only to times when it is absolutely necessary will get you much further than prickly, quarrelsome, combative disruptions. Learning to handle conflict, your own and that of others, is part of being a strong leader and a good conflict-resolution role model for your team.

Effective leaders employ various means of resolving conflict so that the emotional barriers that prevent participants from dealing with the basic issues of their dispute are overcome. Conflict resolution should restore balance, realign relationships and restore productivity to previous or better levels.

Successful Resolution

Although most business dealings have rules or codes of behavior to guide and constrain participants, conflicts do not. It is all too easy for a simple argument to escalate into a fight because our emotions are stirred. Feelings of anger, frustration, fear, rejection, injustice, mistrust and defensiveness come to the surface, clouding judgment and lowering the inhibitions of good manners and polite restraint.

Effective problem-solving must find a way to get people thinking reasonably before dealing with the underlying problems and events that caused the conflict.

Using a logical, step-by-step method of resolution will help.

1. Give supportive, nonjudgmental attention to all parties on neutral ground.

2. Ask questions and listen with empathy until you are able to summarize all points of view in single sentences.

3. Provide incentives for resolving the conflict.

4. State consequences of failing to resolve.

5. Establish rules of procedure so that the most vocal, aggressive or powerful parties do not dominate the discussion.

HANDLING THE BIG FOUR

6. Do not start discussions until all parties are ready to talk.

7. Refuse to allow interruptions, name-calling, etc. that will reduce the discussion to mere conflict again.

Since misunderstandings and poor communication are often the causes of workplace conflict, look into these areas first. Quite often it is only necessary to clear up any misunderstandings, misapprehensions and mistakes to get a resolution that satisfies everyone.

Resolution of business conflicts should:

- Benefit the organization or company
- Provide a win-win solution that benefits all parties
- Prevent future conflict
- Prevent future negative attitudes

An effective leader will train or provide training opportunities for her workers to learn to be good problem-solvers. Workers who have conflict-resolution skills or who are good negotiators will avoid the burden of always being dragged into workplace disputes.

Delegate minor conflicts to team leaders. Conflict resolution is a skill well worth passing on to the whole workforce if possible. People who learn to resolve conflicts at work are also likely to use this skill in their personal lives. Improved personal relationships equal improved worker self-esteem, which means a more highly motivated, more productive worker. Taking time to learn, practice and pass on conflict-resolution skills will benefit you and your company.

Crisis

The end of the 20th century saw a marked increase in the potential for violent disaster. Acts of terrorism, bomb threats, mass shootings, hostage-taking, arson and armed robbery were widely publicized, causing business leaders to begin taking a more proactive stance in crisis-management planning. Many companies became aware of the destructive power of unwanted media attention when involved in litigation, industrial accidents, political scandals and environmental protests.

These major crises need to be addressed through planning. You might be able to help your company by drawing attention to areas where it is vulnerable to future disasters. This includes matters such as poor compliance with safety rules, inattention to the legal requirement of employee-employer relations, or changing building codes. There are many pitfalls. Not all companies take the time necessary to plan for a crisis until after the crisis happens.

Excellence in handling an unexpected crisis can be one of the ways you will get noticed as possible promotion material. The fact that you acted calmly and assertively under a sudden, acute onslaught of new, unexpected, difficult or dangerous activity will not make you a CEO overnight. It will get people in command to notice you and treat you with respect. It might help you to be considered favorably in the future.

Because of insurance or litigation issues, it is not acceptable behavior for an employee to:

- Gossip to outsiders, even your family, about the company's business
- Talk to the media about the company without the express permission of your employer
- Speculate on the cause or lay blame for the crisis on anyone
- Give opinions about the crisis without being sure of the facts

It is acceptable to:

- Pass on information to the media or public that your employer has designated as OK
- To tell people that the company is doing everything it can to deal with the situation

Handling the Big Four

- Tell people that the company is trying to ensure that the problem will not occur again

- Say that the problem is being investigated thoroughly

It is sometimes necessary for very brief periods during a crisis to act in what might otherwise be construed as an aggressive way. Barking out orders, yelling, or even using physical force to get people moving out of danger is acceptable communication in a crisis. Getting people out of a burning building or into a tornado shelter are good examples of when aggressive behavior will be seen positively.

Effective Crisis Management

1. Plan ahead and know what to do when crisis hits.

2. Know where fire escapes and safety equipment are.

3. Train employees to handle potentially dangerous situations.

4. Comply with all applicable safety regulations.

5. Update safety regulations regularly.

6. Apply the most stringent safety codes (for example, those required by any union operating in your company) to all employees.

7. Prepare statements that can be given out to the media as quickly as possible after any disaster hits.

8. Designate spokespersons to deal with the media and establish a no-comment rule for other media/employee communications.

9. Establish proactive methods for dealing with and minimizing the harmful fallout from any crisis.

10. Create policies for crisis management that are compatible with law enforcement and external emergency services.

Having policies in place to handle major emergencies, natural disasters or accidents is good company practice. If your company does not have a crisis-management team, bring the topic to the fore at the next opportunity.

No matter how well the company is prepared, however, small, less dramatic events or miniature disasters do crop up and cause problems. Women are often good at calming or soothing others in dangerous situations. They are less likely to inflame a dangerous situation by unwanted heroics or enraging an irrational criminal. A cool, quiet demeanor or giving assistance until proper emergency help arrives and preventing a bad situation from getting worse are usually what are required in most emergencies.

In our society, expert help is usually available within a short time when most disasters hit. Prepare yourself by building your self-esteem. Self-confident people are usually good at handling problems. They feel that they can be depended upon to do the right thing, and that is what they do. Believe in yourself. Act assertively and you will be able to handle a crisis with the best of them. All this communicates leadership ability.

Criticism

Giving Criticism or Feedback on Performance

When your job calls upon you to let workers know that there are problems with the way they are doing the job, you'll probably dread confronting them with the news. Some supervisors avoid evaluations or employee assessments simply because they feel uncomfortable criticizing others. Many women are reluctant to give criticism, even when it is completely deserved, because they do not want to damage a relationship or hurt the other person's feelings.

Challenging poor performance and promoting the necessary changes to make the worker more productive are supervisory activities. Failure to make clear the nature and effects of poor or unacceptable performance leads to confusion and resentment. Remember that people often take silence as agreement. Unless you tell them that there is a problem, most workers will either not know the problem exists or think that you do not care enough to get it changed. Responsibility for poor performance will be seen by the worker as yours, since you were in charge but did nothing to make it better.

HANDLING THE BIG FOUR

**What to Do When You Are Tempted to Do Nothing,
But Know You Must Act**

Change the name — start thinking in terms of helpful feedback rather than criticism. Tell workers that you wish to give them some feedback on performance and that you will be looking for their input and ideas on ways to make things better.

List problem areas in a clear, unambiguous way. Do not exaggerate or minimize problems. Do not blame. Avoid criticizing personalities or making statements that suggest the person has not met acceptable standards because of stupidity or that otherwise demean or belittle the worker.

Ask for, and take seriously, suggestions from the worker. Have suggestions for improving performance ready to offer. Discuss and resolve the situation by coming up with a plan or program for the worker to try that the worker accepts as viable. The more heavily involved with formulation the worker has been, the more likely it is that the plan will be successful.

Tackling problems by giving feedback as soon as things start to deteriorate, and well before bad habits and attitudes have been established, will make them easier to handle. Be fair. Listen to explanations and treat everyone the same. Telling people that poor performance from them reflects badly on co-workers or the whole team is often a good motivator.

Find motivators for change that fit the individual. Do not make threats you cannot carry out. Do not promise rewards you cannot give.

Workers who are poorly or insufficiently trained cannot possibly do a good job. Provide training, coaching or mentoring for those in need.

Employees who undergo regular evaluations and performance reviews will probably handle feedback better than those who are unused to them. Establishing a system of performance evaluation, which includes self-assessment, will actually reduce the burden of having to criticize. Employees who are accustomed to looking at their performance and who are motivated to constantly review and improve their methods are more likely to continue a high level of productivity and stay better motivated than those who simply wait to be told what to do. They assume more responsibility for their actions and are more likely to notice problems before they develop. They will also be vigilant to maintain team performance and give feedback to fellow team members when things are getting lax.

Women are often reluctant to give criticism because they fear rejection. You are not in business to be popular! The truth remains that respecting is more important than liking when it comes to being an effective manager. The higher you climb up the corporate ladder, the more important it is to be respected than to be liked.

Taking Criticism or Feedback From Others

Step 1. Put It in Perspective

One reason why women hate giving criticism is that we know how much we dislike being on the receiving end. The lower your self-esteem, the more you dislike criticism.

Norma Carr-Ruffino in *The Promotable Woman* has a good illustration for the way in which we take criticism. It is not directed only at women, but if taking criticism well is a problem for you, it can be illuminating.

She uses the automatic piloting and navigational equipment on planes as her example. These machines talk to each other constantly as the autopilot instructs the navigation device to make necessary adjustments to get the plane to its destination. The navigation equipment never gets resentful, even though the adjustments it must make are constantly being drawn to its attention. If two people were doing the work, they would almost certainly end up in an altercation because the navigator would take the pilot's calls for adjustment as criticisms of his or her work. It is because we take the criticism personally and see it as reflecting badly upon ourselves that we have trouble accepting it well.

When people criticize you in a harsh, negative manner, you are bound to feel hurt and offended. Letting go of hurt feelings and refusing to allow the negative opinions of others undermine your self-esteem is good, assertive

HANDLING THE BIG FOUR

behavior, hard to do but well worth attempting. You can let the unwarranted criticism spoil your day or deliberately put it out of your mind. The choice is yours.

Put the criticism into perspective through logical evaluation.

Ask yourself how worthy the critical person is to offer criticism to you in the first place.

- Is the person someone you respect?
- Is the critical person an expert in the field?
- Does this person understand your motivation, goals or vision?
- Could the criticizer do a better job him or herself?

If the answers to these questions are no, then why are you listening to or concerned about the criticism in the first place? Put-downs or unwarranted criticism from ill-informed people are not worth considering seriously or getting upset over.

If the answer to any of these questions is yes, then ask another question.

- How much does the critical person's opinion matter?

If it does not matter, then you will be less concerned than if it does. Criticism from someone we love or respect is hard to take. Surprise attacks from those we consider friends or supporters are also especially difficult.

Criticism from an expert in the field who understands your goals, motivation and vision, who could do a better job and/or whose opinion matters, warrants your attention. Justified criticism should not be brushed aside.

Step 2. Learn From It

If you can learn to do so, avoid taking criticism personally and start learning from it. Use criticism as feedback on your performance. Let it motivate you to learn more, develop your abilities and learn new skills.

If you dislike the way criticism was given, let the other person know by a direct, factual statement that you do not appreciate being put down, sniped at or being the target of unfair, inaccurate remarks. When people criticize, apply the criticism to the action, job, idea or any other thing rather than apply it to yourself.

> e.g., "The idea seemed a good one to me at the time, and I still believe it has merit. I'm sorry that you dislike it so much, or perhaps we could make some adjustments to make it work for you. Do you want me to start over, or shall I wait for you to get back to me with your suggestion?"

When we take criticism personally, we lose our assertive control of the situation. We look unprofessional and nobody respects us; we don't even respect ourselves.

> e.g., "What do you mean you don't like my idea. I suppose you think it's stupid. You probably think I'm stupid too. Well, I don't have to take this sort of criticism from you or anybody. I'm leaving, and you can handle the project yourself."

A really effective way to handle negative criticism is to say something like, "Thanks for the input" or "Thanks for bringing the problem to my attention."

A refusal to accept the criticism personally or be upset by it is a strong response to people who are trying to put you down or undermine your position.

If the critical person was really offensive, then by all means tell them that you appreciate honest feedback but do not appreciate their manner of delivery. Don't pretend that it doesn't matter to you if it really does. Bottled-up emotions cause stress-related illness, such as heart disease and high blood pressure. Accept that your feelings are hurt or upset and choose to respond to those feelings immediately to those involved or later by yourself.

- Let others know that you will not accept unfair or unwarranted criticism.

- Clear the air by expressing your feelings.

- Do not carry around resentment or plot revenge.

Handling the Big Four

- Talk things over with a mentor or trusted friend.
- Do not tell yourself or let others tell you your feelings are wrong.

If you are afraid that overwhelming feelings will hamper your ability to stay calm and objective, delay expressing them to others until later.

Turn your objections to the behavior meted out to you by others into feedback for them. Instruct them in how to give constructive feedback properly. Let them know that they have acted inappropriately. Far from reacting angrily as many others would, you will help them overcome their poor skills in giving feedback so that they will not make such mistakes in the future.

Remember, there are people who will use criticism as a weapon to humiliate you and put you down. These people are bullies and intimidators. You don't have to take criticism from such individuals to heart. Confrontation is a choice you can make.

Keep reminding yourself:

- You are a valuable person.
- You do not rely on the validation or approval of others to feel accepted and worthwhile.
- Your strength comes from within, from knowing that you are a strong, dynamic professional.
- Others cannot force you into making choices you do not want to make.
- Others cannot put you down unless you allow them to do so.

Compliments

In some ways compliments are harder to handle gracefully than criticism. Some women might be wary of compliments and feel that the compliment giver is insincere or has an ulterior motive for being nice. Some men might use flattery to get sexual favors from women, so a certain amount of distrust can be expected. However, in business, take the words of praise at face value unless you are absolutely positive that they're insincere.

Many women feel so uncomfortable with praise and admiration that they do not know what to say to the compliment giver.

Beware of gushing! A smile and brief "Thank you" are quite sufficient. If the compliment is given in a meeting or group, a smile and nod to acknowledge the remark will do. You might want to add some comment later after the meeting. Say something like, "I really appreciated your support in there, Betty, thanks." Letting people know that their words meant something to you is fine. You might perhaps say, "Thanks for the compliment, Bob. This is a new dress, and I hoped it would look good. You've made my day."

Women sometimes make the mistake of trying to reciprocate a compliment, so that when Joan compliments them on their dress, they feel compelled to admire Joan's clothes in return. This can lead to you being the one making phony compliments if there is really nothing very admirable about Joan's wardrobe. It's better to accept your compliment with a smile and a word of thanks and wait for an opportunity to repay the compliment later at a more opportune time.

Some people receive a compliment with self-deprecation. Do you do this? Think back to the last time that someone said something especially nice to you. Did you disclaim the compliment instead of accepting it?

> e.g., Jean responds to Bob's nice words about the new dress with a lie, to negate her pleasure in the compliment. Instead of smiling thanks, she says, "Oh this old thing, I've had it for years, but it's too comfortable to throw out." She goes on to tell Bob that he was mistaken in his admiration by saying, "I shouldn't wear this color. It makes me look washed-out."

If someone gives you a compliment, accept it. Compliments are great morale boosters, especially when they really are deserved. If you've done a good job, you deserve a compliment. If you look neat and elegant and someone notices, be happy about it.

HANDLING THE BIG FOUR

If you receive a compliment for work in which others were involved, or which you had delegated to another, then acknowledge it at once.

> e.g., "Thank you for your compliment, Ms. Granger, but I was only one of a team involved in the project. I'll pass on your comments to the others, unless you would rather see them yourself."
>
> Or say, "Excuse me for interrupting, Ms. Granger, but as much as I'd like to accept your compliment, it should really be given to Bill and Kate. They were the ones who undertook the project. They did a great job, and I think that they deserve to get the praise."

Stealing credit, praise and compliments unfairly is deplorable behavior that causes employees to become resentful of managers and supervisors. It also undermines you by making you look like a one-man band, rather than a strong leader of a strong team.

What do you do about the man who keeps paying you excessive compliments? Some men are prone to pay compliments compulsively. Start by assessing the situation. Ask yourself how important the problem really is to you.

1. Does the behavior bother you enough to want it stopped? If you want to end all such future compliments, give a firm I-message and follow up by ignoring any future remarks.

2. Is it sexual harassment? If the remarks constitute sexual harassment, then document the incidents and file a complaint. Personal remarks about your body are not permissible.

3. Is it unimportant? If you know that it's just old Herb shooting his mouth off again, if the remarks are not abusive or offensive, and if it really is not important, turn it into a joke. Say something like, "That's right, Herb, I'm wonderful," and walk away. Do not smile, just look bored. Herb will soon get tired of trying to make you blush or feel uncomfortable.

When a Compliment Becomes Sexual Harassment

Always support employees who complain about sexual harassment. Good documentation and reporting through channels are the proper procedures. Companies that do not follow through to discipline harassers are increasingly likely to be held liable if employees file suit. Most large companies have sexual-harassment policies in place. See your human resources manager if you're having problems and get the problem out in the open. If your company does not have a policy, you might want to consider being the person who instigates setting one in place.

Use Compliments to Build Your Dynamic Energy

Mark Twain once said, "An occasional compliment is necessary to keep up one's self-respect ... When you cannot get a compliment any other way, pay yourself one."

Remember Twain's words if you want your workplace to energize you. Many people complain of being drained by their work. Dynamic leaders report just the opposite. They are able to use the things that happen at work, good and bad, to learn and grow by and to make themselves stronger.

Use the good things to build yourself up and then work on ways of learning and growing through the bad times. People who do not let themselves benefit from the good times are twice as likely to end up feeling drained and powerless. They do not even have the good stuff like praise and compliments to build them up.

Notice that Mark Twain uses the word "pay" to describe giving a compliment. In the past, compliments were always paid. If you have trouble accepting compliments, it is good to keep this in mind next time you get one. It is easier to accept payment for something that has been earned.

Positive Self-Talk

The idea of giving yourself a compliment sounds silly at first. Instead of calling it a compliment, think of it as positive self-talk. Research studies show

Handling the Big Four

that positive self-talk is a wonderful way to build self-esteem and improve the attitude. Negative attitudes hold people back from realizing their full potential.

Negative self-talk is much more common than the positive kind. Most people, men as well as women, carry around a load of negative put-downs from the past. Learning to let go of them is hard. Practicing positive self-talk is one way of combating your internal negative put-downs that hamper your ability to be as dynamic and powerful as you would like.

Some examples of negative self-talk are:

- "I'm too fat."
- "I'm too stupid to learn the new computer program."
- "Nobody listens to me."
- "People treat me like a doormat."
- "I'm selfish to want my own way."

A good start to planning positive self-talk messages to replace the negative ones is to list your perennial favorites. We all have them. Make a list of yours. Leave a space beside or underneath each one. When the list is finished, write positive disclaimers in the spaces beside them. Copy your new list onto a separate sheet of paper and destroy the one with negative comments.

Positive disclaimers for our list above might be:

- "I am comfortable with my weight."
- "I can learn anything I set my mind to."
- "People listen to what I say."
- "I am an assertive person. People treat me with respect."
- "My needs are as important as the needs of others."

Use your positive disclaimer list every day. Even if it makes you feel self-conscious at first, saying the list aloud to yourself while looking in the mirror is an excellent way of starting to make yourself believe the positive rather than the negative self-talk statements. Say the positive disclaimer to yourself every time a negative thought creeps into your mind. Add compliments and praise remarks from others to the bottom of your list for an extra ego boost.

REFLECTIONS

Reflections on Handling Conflict, Crisis, Criticism and Compliments

Make up an I-message that allows you to respond assertively to each of the big-four challenges. Remember,

- When you …
- I feel …
- Because …
- I prefer …

Conflict cannot be resolved until all parties step back from the emotional turmoil and agree to seek a win-win solution. Think of a conflict that you are in — at work, home or socially. Use the space below to write down your I-message. When you finish your message, practice saying it aloud to yourself or to a friend. Evaluate the statement to make sure it is as effective and assertive as necessary. Make adjustments until you are satisfied

- When you …

- I feel …

- Because …

- I prefer …

Reflections

REFLECTIONS

Crises are best handled by careful forethought and planning. Crisis-management teams are the modern, effective way to prepare for possible future problems or disasters of all kinds.

Imagine that your company or department does not have crisis-response systems set up and think how you would get people in charge to put them in place. Compose an effective I-message that will get the crisis-management ball rolling in your company or department. (Note the slight variation in the message for this example.)

- When you …

- I feel …

- Because …

- I prefer (suggest) …

Reflections

Criticism is painful, especially if you feel it is unwarranted. Imagine that a peer from another department has criticized your latest project, saying that you did not put enough work into it and that it was sloppily done. Compose an I-message that will let the person know that you are not taking the remarks personally, that you appreciate the attempt to give input, but that you do not believe your peer is experienced enough to give effective criticism.

- When you …

- I feel …

- Because …

- I prefer (suggest) …

Reflections

Compliments are good for your self-esteem. Take them at face value with thanks. But they can be damaging and destructive. Imagine that a male co-worker is continually paying you inappropriate compliments. Use an I-message to tell him to stop.

- When you …

- I feel …

- Because …

- I prefer (suggest) …

Reflections

6 EFFECTIVE WRITING

Everything you write is an opportunity to make a good impression on your reader, whether that reader is a co-worker, a colleague in another company, a customer or your boss. If your writing contains mistakes, your reader will think that you are careless and illiterate.

Before you begin writing, make sure that you are using the best medium for communication.

Is Writing the Best Medium?

Whether you are writing by letter, memo, report, e-mail, note or fax, ask yourself if the medium you've chosen is the best possible under the circumstances. Writing is not always the best way to communicate. Sometimes it is better to go face-to-face. The telephone could be quicker and simpler. Communicating by the most effective method is the way to look efficient and in control.

Think about the reason you are making this particular communication. That will help you to decide if writing is the best medium.

It is best to write when:

- Confirming an oral agreement
- Formalizing a business transaction

- Recording minutes of a meeting

- Documenting problems, disciplinary actions, suggestions for future reference

- Submitting a formal report

- Submitting a proposal or project plan

- Ensuring that others do not take credit for your new ideas

- Building goodwill

Remember: It is important to send handwritten notes of condolence, thanks and congratulations. Handwritten replies to invitations are also a nice touch.

It's still customary to write, date and sign formal agreements. Putting it in writing is sound business. It avoids confusion and errors and gives a point of reference for future transactions. Deals are less likely to go wrong when they are properly documented. Since most people have an imperfect memory, people carry away different impressions from the same event. A written record that all agree upon will prevent things getting forgotten or distorted from one meeting to the next.

Documentation is very important. Legal action or formal disciplinary procedures such as suspension or firing cannot happen without good documentation of the incidents. Harassment, tardiness or inattention to warnings must be documented or the insubordinate person might claim improper termination and seek redress.

It has been rightly said that memos are not made to inform the recipient but to protect the sender. If you have a new idea or proposal, putting it in a memo to your boss before talking to anyone about it will help you get the credit later. Get your side of the story down first if you believe someone is going to make a damaging complaint about you.

Put it in writing if it is your duty to warn your boss that safety violations or labor laws are being broken. This way you cannot be blamed later when ignoring laws and rules ends in a crisis or disaster. Make notes if there is a

EFFECTIVE WRITING

crisis or accident in your department. Immediate impressions are important, so write them down immediately. Include names of witnesses or have them cosign the report. With good documentation, you might save your company a lot of money or help get fair compensation for an employee.

Write down evaluations and follow-up assessments of your projects, with suggestions for the next time you tackle something similar. Memory alone will be insufficient to keep you from avoiding similar pitfalls or improving past performance.

When you are sure that putting it in writing is the best medium for your message, and you know what needs to be said, it is time to move ahead.

You need to know three things to be an effective writer. You need to know:

1. What you want to say

2. Who you want to say it to

3. How to say it correctly

Know What You Want to Say

Knowing your subject is very important. If you are unsure about your topic, learn more before you write about it so that you do not make foolish mistakes.

Sometimes, you may know your subject so well that you forget your reader does not know it at the same level. Remember:

- Avoid unnecessary jargon or technical language, especially if you are unsure that you, or the recipient, know the meaning of the words.

- Acronyms and initials are permissible as long as the whole words have a first reference.

- Do not try your audience's patience with long descriptions. Make a rough draft, if you are unsure, and then prune the unnecessary parts. Most writers tend to put in too much information rather than too little. If the recipients want more information, they will write or call back and request it later.

Who Are Your Readers, and How Should They Be Addressed?

This is an important question because a skilled writer will try to slant her writing to make the best impression on the reader. This is even more important when writing to authority figures.

- Some people are impatient and intolerant of a verbose, flowery style. Use brief sentences, plenty of short, action words and bulleted or point-form lists rather than long, descriptive sentences. Write concisely for this person until you are adept at sending the brief, pointed notes that will get read and not be tossed impatiently into the trash.

- Some older bosses are quite pedantic. They will be annoyed or scornful of poor grammar or spelling errors. They want proper business usage in your letters and do not appreciate notes without a proper salutation or that contain abbreviations or slang. Please this audience by getting a good business grammar book and learning to do it right before you send another letter.

- Use the spell-check and grammar function on your computer.

- Use your dictionary.

- Proofread what you write or what a secretary writes for you.

- There is no excuse for poor writing that irritates the reader.

EFFECTIVE WRITING

If you are unsure of the audience — perhaps because you're writing to a new client in another city or if several people will read what you've written — choose a style that is as simple and straightforward as possible.

Here's a quick way to determine how difficult your writing is for the reader to understand. Communications experts tell us that the formula to use when judging the simplicity of your writing style is to take 150 words of what you have written and count up the number of one-syllable words. Divide this number by 10 and subtract it from 20. The remainder equals the number of years of schooling a person must have had to be able to understand what you have written.

When you are unsure of the reading ability of your business audience, aim at a style that has around 100-115 single-syllable words per 150 words of text. Similarly, the less sure you are of your audience, the fewer technical terms or jargon words you can use.

Keep the following in mind when thinking of your audience:

- Today's readers won't struggle through difficult written messages.
- North Americans tend to be even less patient than other nationalities, especially the young.
- Asian and some European people tend to be more patient and better able to cope with copious information; however, that is not an excuse to write long-winded, dull letters to clients in Asia or Europe.

Choose Your Style to Send an Unwritten Message Along With the Written Words

Using:

- Short sentences
- Brief paragraphs
- Bullet-style presentation
- Numbered points

Indicates that you are:

- Being brief and businesslike
- Not wanting to waste the reader's time
- Aware that the reader has more important things to do
- Acting more like an equal than a subordinate

Using:

- Pros and cons
- Several different suggestions
- Suggestions of alternate solutions
- Future outcome possibilities

Indicates that:

- You have thought about this topic carefully
- That you are aware that the decision does not rest with you alone
- You value the opinion of the reader
- The reader need not waste time forming conclusions you have already reached

Using:

- Examples of benefits for the reader
- Examples of benefits for yourself
- Specific examples of what you want

Indicates that:

- You want to get cooperation from the reader

EFFECTIVE WRITING

- You have thought out the situation thoroughly
- You are assertive

Using:

- Contractions when they sound right
- An informal style
- Phrases that sound like you speaking

Indicates that:

- You are a peer
- Neither you nor the reader is a stuffy, formal person
- You and the reader have a good, open, working relationship

Timing Is Everything

Writing used to be a fairly slow method of business communication. Today, the fax machine or computer can take a written message and deliver it as quickly as making a phone call. This is a great advantage in a lot of instances. Modern business thrives in an atmosphere of haste. We live in a world that values speed and is frustrated easily by having to wait in line or wait for an answer.

However, it has been wisely said that the more important the message, the slower should be its method of delivery. Snap decisions are not always best. Sometimes it is best to take time to think. Writing can help you get ideas clear in your mind. It can help you sort out things logically. Flaws in logic are easier to spot when an argument is written rather than spoken.

Have you often heard someone say at the end of a phone call, "Please send me a written outline of that, will you? I want to study it a bit longer."

The written word has a power that the spoken lacks. It is easier to prove libel than slander, because the written word leaves evidence. Be careful of what you write and read it before sending to ensure that you have not said something that is inappropriate. Many companies have statements to the media or to the public checked by their legal department before sending them. Hasty, angry or accusing words are hard to recall once written.

Don't write when you are annoyed or upset. Take time to simmer down. It is better to delay the response until you have slept on it and had some sober second thoughts. If you still have doubts about the wisdom of what you have written, get a person you trust to check it for you.

Effective Writing

Use the EFFECTIVE acronym to help you remember some of the important tips for writing business communications well.

Establish that writing is the best medium for your message.

Find out all you need to know about your topic.

Frame your message to fit the audience.

Establish the reason for communicating this way.

Control the urge to write when angry or upset.

Take time to check your writing for errors.

Impress your reader by your excellent writing skills.

Vary your style to suit your audience.

Express yourself with clarity and brevity and avoid jargon and pretentious language.

EFFECTIVE WRITING

How to Say It Correctly

You cannot afford to make a grammar mistake in your writing. Get a good grammar guide and keep it next to your desk. If in doubt — always look it up! Never, ever take a chance on leaving a mistake in your message. If you can't find an answer in your grammar guide, change the sentence or wording to a format that you're sure is correct.

Similarly, always use the spell check on your computer. No matter how short the correspondence, errors creep in — even after you've proofread the material several times. Familiarity with the material creates a blind spot in our proofreading. If you don't have spell check, then ask a colleague to look it over quickly.

Finally, proofread again. Read it word by word so that each word stands alone. You'll be surprised at how many little mistakes you'll catch that your grammar and spelling programs didn't. For example, the words "if," "is," "it" and "in" are all correct words, but not if they're in a sentence like this:

"I believe that our best interests lie is refunding the customer."

Did you catch the error? It's not that easy to see. Any spell check would say that this sentence is correct.

REFLECTIONS

Reflections on EFFECTIVE Writing

Find five examples of correspondence that you have written recently. Analyze them using the following questions:

1. Was writing the best medium for this communication? Why or why not?

2. Who is my audience? What do I know about them? Did my writing style suit this audience?

3. What did I want to say to my reader? Did I keep it short, simple and straightforward? Did my reader get my message?

4. Is this correct? Have I missed any errors? Spelling? Grammar? Anything else?

Based on your answers, what changes do you need to make to your writing?

7 TELEPHONE TECHNIQUES

Telephone Negatives

The telephone is such a part of our lives that it is hard to imagine not having it. But it is also intrusive and demanding and seldom connects us with the person we want when we want them. This is the age of being on hold, voice mail, call-waiting and telephone tag.

It is also the age of cellular phones and the relatively new phenomenon of "cell rage." Interruptions, poor driving and disregard for others by cell phone users have infuriated so many people that violent altercations and cell-phone destruction can result.

Call-waiting and other interruptions that involve being put on hold are annoying, especially when the other person was the one who called you. Listening to music you hate or boring advertisements for the other company's products seem to make the wait longer and harder to endure than silence. A bout of telephone tag can end up taking longer than if you had sent a letter.

DYNAMIC COMMUNICATION SKILLS FOR WOMEN

Three Ways to Win the Telephone Battle

1. **Help Yourself by Learning More**

    It's a good idea to learn some tips for using the telephone assertively so that you don't end up feeling victimized, angry and upset, or that your life is being ruled by something outside your control. Like fire, the telephone is a terrific servant but a bad master. Mastering the use of the phone will help you feel in control.

    If you have a telephone system that involves several lines and services such as hold, switching to another line, making recordings, and putting onto speaker, learn how to do them properly. Write down the instructions and follow them carefully until the procedures become second nature. This is especially important if you don't always handle the phone. Supervisors should be able to use equipment in an emergency or simply because they want to. You could look or at least feel foolish if you had to ask an employee how to use the phone in your departmental office.

2. **Wind Up the Windbags**

    Another problem for many involves getting away gracefully from telephone bores. These people waste your time by gabbing on about trivial matters rather than getting to the point and telling you why they called. It is even worse at the end of the call when the business is over but they won't say goodbye!

    Sam Horne, author of *Tongue Fu*, has some good tips for dealing with windbags. She suggests that the windbag time-wasters are really bullying types. They don't care about you or your needs. The assertive person realizes that her needs are as important as those of the other person. Ms. Horne suggests using a firm interruption of the monologue by saying the other person's name to get their attention and stop the flow. Then, without giving the windbag time to start again, give a brief reiteration of the past conversation and sign off. Say something like,

TELEPHONE TECHNIQUES

"Mr. French, thanks for the information on wing nuts. I'm going to mail you a confirming letter today about the proposal. I know you're a very busy man, and I don't want to take up any more of your time. I appreciate your information. Goodbye for now." Click.

This type of finish is polite, firm and can be made whenever there is a lull in the monologue long enough to insert the first word. Once started on your farewell speech, DO NOT STOP. It can also be adapted to suit personal callers, family members or friends and has a dual benefit. It ends the call without giving offense and leaves you feeling empowered and in control.

3. Win on the Phone to Build Your Assertiveness Muscles

Winning small battles produces feelings of power that build us up and leave us feeling good about ourselves. When we cope with a stressor such as the telephone time-waster positively, we experience eustress — the good stress — that builds our self-esteem, rather than distress — the bad stress — that lowers it.

The telephone needs to be a useful tool for us to help us do business better. All too often, it is a tyrant. We shudder when it rings but cannot avoid answering. Learn to handle the telephone well and avoid being distressed by its insistent, frustrating qualities.

Thirty Tips for Effective Telephone Usage

1. While on hold, do small jobs, such as reading mail and clearing computer files.

2. If you spend a lot of time on the phone, free up your hands with a shoulder rest.

3. If you have privacy, use the speaker. Inform a caller that the speaker is on if others can overhear.

DYNAMIC COMMUNICATION SKILLS FOR WOMEN

4. Know and use time-saving features such as re-dial and auto-dial.

5. Have a card for calls outside the office.

6. Make sure that a simple phone call is the best medium for conveying your message. A letter or conference call best handles complex items, things that will need time for the other party to consider or that involve several people's input.

7. Don't leave long complex messages with people who are not directly involved in your business.

8. Don't leave voice mail that should not be heard by a third party.

9. Call at sensible times and check for time-zone changes before dialing. Know your audience so that you only make those networking or keeping in touch type of calls when the other party is not likely to be extremely busy.

10. Check voice mail frequently. Reply to messages promptly.

11. Don't eat, drink, smoke or laugh and chat to others while talking on the phone.

12. Don't call when you're angry or upset.

13. Ask permission before placing people on hold.

14. Give options to call back or leave messages if you know the hold will be lengthy.

15. Take messages for others with correct times, dates and names but avoid long, involved messages containing information that does not concern you.

16. Deliver messages taken for others promptly.

17. Give your name at the start of the call to avoid confusion.

18. Use your company name immediately after your own when making a business call.

TELEPHONE TECHNIQUES

19. Spend a short time only on salutations, greetings and personal chat. Always assume that the other person is twice as busy as you are and maintain a professional atmosphere by avoiding unnecessary chatter.

20. Have all the information, documents and files on your desk or ready for access on the computer before beginning an important call.

21. Walk around while talking. It gives you exercise and increases the circulation of blood to the brain to stimulate thought.

22. Delegate calls that you don't need to make personally.

23. Group calls together, checking off the list and noting who has to be called back to avoid omissions.

24. Do not allow calls to interrupt you during appointments.

25. If you know you must take an exceptionally important call during a meeting, tell everyone present and apologize beforehand.

26. Don't allow your cell phone to interrupt or annoy others.

27. Keep personal calls at the office brief.

28. Call to confirm appointments the day before if possible.

29. Call to apologize if you are unavoidably late or unable to meet your schedule.

30. Follow up the call, and when necessary, with written confirmation.

REFLECTIONS

Reflections on Telephone Techniques

Getting off the phone gracefully at the end of a business call can be tricky. Many women allow their concern for the feelings of the other person to override their need to be brief and businesslike. Learning how to exit easily will let the other person recognize you as a professional person who knows what she wants and has her priorities straight. You are, after all, there to work, not chat.

Take the Telephone Challenge

Use the space below to compose a good farewell speech that you can use to fill that awkward gap between finishing the business part of the call and saying, "Goodbye."

Remember, your aim is to:

- Be friendly and polite.
- Be brief.
- Acknowledge the value of the call.
- Recognize that the other party has time constraints.
- Express your own time constraints.
- End on an upbeat note.

Aim for a message of no more than 20 words; 10-15 words would be better.

8 DYNAMIC PRESENTATIONS

Stage fright affects almost everyone when asked to speak in public. Famous people, actors, politicians, teachers, preachers and even talk-show hosts all suffer butterflies when they have to speak to an audience. This feeling does not go away with time. It may get worse, in fact, especially if previous attempts at giving a speech, performance or presentation went badly. Stage fright includes such symptoms as sweaty palms, trembling knees, a queasy stomach, elevated blood pressure, nausea, sleeplessness, anxiety and loss of appetite.

Most Americans will describe the thought of having to speak in public as something they loathe. As a result, most presentations given in a business setting are boring, embarrassing and badly done.

Public Speaking Is Stressful

A fear of public speaking is in the top 10 most stressful events, according to analysts of women in business.

The fear is linked closely with fears of:

- Being center stage with everybody's attention focused on you
- The unknown

- Making mistakes or looking foolish in front of others
- Loss of self-esteem

It takes effort and expertise to speak well publicly. If your job requires you to do a lot of presentations or if you plan to move into that area as your career develops, it is wise to prepare by training yourself now.

Giving a good presentation is an empowering, positive experience. The euphoria of having come through with flying colors can make you want to rush out and celebrate or at least bask in the glow of success. A bad presentation might make you want to run and hide, vowing never to think about the awful experience again.

Both these attitudes are unhelpful if you want to grow your abilities and become better in the future. Always take time soon after the presentation to evaluate. Note what went well and what went wrong. Learning from experience is the best teacher of all.

> *"Public speaking success is not the result of eliminating those butterflies from your stomach, but simply getting them to fly in formation."*
>
> — Toastmasters International

Many performers will tell you that nervousness before a performance can be excruciating but that they feel that they work better when they experience stage fright. Nerves then are not the real problem; they should not prevent us from presenting well, but spur us on to do better.

What can be done to ensure that we will make a good presentation despite our quite natural nervousness over speaking in public?

Ten Factors for Making a Dynamic Presentation

1. Know your topic — the rule of thumb is three pages of information in your head for every page of notes. You don't have to say it all but be ready for questions with extra facts.

Dynamic Presentations

2. Know your audience — have at least an idea of the number of people you expect to be there and who those people will be.

3. Give the audience what they want — meeting audience expectations is important to retaining their goodwill and keeping them listening.

4. Keep it brief — adult attention spans are in the 20-minute range, and the younger the audience, the shorter the span.

5. Keep it simple — use short, colorful words and an expressive tone as much as possible. Avoid jargon and technical terms unless all of the audience can understand. A lot of figures and facts will not be remembered after just one hearing.

6. Use visual aids — these help people understand and remember what you say. Charts, diagrams, slides, overheads, handouts, computer programs, video, photographs and drawings will help get your point across quicker and easier than spoken words.

7. Entertain and inform, together if possible — most people recall things they enjoyed learning much better than those they did not. Stories, jokes, examples and anecdotes, as long as they are well used and appropriate, will help if the information is heavy or lighten the gloom if the news is bad.

8. Inspire — Americans are very responsive to inspirational or challenging messages. One way of handling a speech in which bad news must be given is to look for positive, inspirational aspects of the situation to help people find ways to cope.

9. Concentrate — it is easy to become distracted by people in the audience or activity outside the room and lose your train of thought.

10. Prepare and practice — it is not a good idea to memorize your talk. If you are comfortable about speaking without notes, then by all means do so, but it is better to read your speech well than repeat it word for word. Memory can let you down, and if you get

interrupted or distracted, you may be unable to carry on from that point again. Use notes to remind you of your points and use them as anchors to assist you as you speak.

Preparation Pointers

- Dress comfortably and wear supportive shoes that will help you stand with good posture.

- Practice standing with your feet apart, one hand easily by your side, the other holding your notes. Stand in front of the mirror and repeat fairy stories or nursery rhymes to your reflection until the stance feels natural. Women tend to fidget and move around too much when they speak. This is jokingly referred to among professional speakers as making it harder to hit a moving target, but it can be distracting for the audience. If you are speaking from your seat at a meeting, for instance, you will have no room to move about. You will also be even more likely to fiddle with papers, lean on the table, shift from foot to foot or kick your chair, unless you have trained yourself to be still.

- Have your notes and visual aids in order and keep any books or reference materials that you have brought along — just in case you need them — neatly stacked to one side. It spoils your continuity and causes delays if you have to stop and scrabble in your briefcase for some additional figures in the middle of a report.

- Check for yourself that the equipment works before the meeting starts. Visual aids that require equipment such as overhead projectors, computer links or even simple flip charts require preparation to ensure they work as planned. If a bulb goes or the power is down, do you have a backup plan so your presentation can continue? Set out handouts at each place before you start to speak, if you can. If handouts should not be seen before a certain point in your presentation, then arrange for someone to hand them out for you. Presentations to clients are often done using electronic equipment. Know how it works and what backup material you need. Sometimes women make the mistake of always relying on a technician to set up their presentation for them. What happens if the technician is sick or delayed? Having to ask your prospective client for pens or a new overhead bulb is not only embarrassingly unprofessional, but will fluster you and spoil your ability to present effectively.

- Eat sensibly and look in the mirror before the presentation starts. You may feel too nervous to eat but be careful. Stomach growls will raise a smile even if your opening joke doesn't. Try to eat something to give you energy before you start. Have a glass of water with lemon and no ice on hand while speaking to combat dry throat and coughing. If your meeting is in the afternoon, eat lunch carefully. Avoid food that might splatter your clothing or cause indigestion. A Canadian radio announcer tells the story of having to greet and interview a famous, glamorous film star after a large Italian lunch. His excitement turned to horror when first his lunch fell into his lap and then his open words of effusive greeting were preceded by a huge, unexpected belch right in the poor woman's face.

- Look around as you talk. Eye contact indicates that you are assured and confident. Try to find a friendly face. Smile, as long as the topic allows it, and use calm open gestures. Visualize the audience as friendly and eager to listen. Concentrating on giving them the information they need to hear will prevent you thinking about yourself and feeling nervous and self-conscious.

- Know your opening sentence. Once you get started, it gets easier to keep going. If you can't start, you'll never get going.

- Don't sweat the small stuff. Skipping a point or pausing to remember isn't the end of the world. It will make you sound more natural and might make your audience more sympathetic. Forgotten points can be brought up later, or they may be covered by questions. Ending with a question period is a good idea, but if there are no questions forthcoming, you may feel awkward about the timing of drawing things to a close. Prepare by having one or two short questions handy yourself. Say something like, "You may have wondered if all our customers were happy with the new package color?" or "Some clients have asked me about next year's design, and in case you are also wondering, it will be … ." This may trigger some further questions from the audience or give them time to think of something they wanted to ask. Otherwise, you can, after a brief pause, end quite legitimately by using a tried-and-true closing phrase like, "Thank you for your attention. If there are no further questions, I will sit down."

- Confront the fear. Make a written list of your fears. Ask yourself what the worst thing is that could happen and get it down on paper. Tear up your list, burn it or flush it.

- Give yourself positive self-talk messages that say you can do a good job. Address your fears and doubts that are causing negative messages to be sent to your mind. Counter those negative thoughts with positive ones. Visualize yourself doing well and being successful.

First You've Got to Get Their Attention

Get the audience seated and facing you before you begin your talk. Chat with people, ask them to find a chair and move around the room if necessary to shepherd them into place. Don't try to yell over their talking or start before they're listening. Once your audience is seated, stand and wait without speaking until everyone is quiet and focused on you. Look around at the audience with a friendly, open expression or slight smile, and then hit them like a ton of bricks.

Begin with an opening that:

- Establishes rapport

- Gets them on your side

Dynamic Presentations

- Piques their interest
- Makes them want to hear more

The tone and style of your talk should be evident from your opening statement.

- Take a major point from the meat of your topic and make that your opening line.
- Give a piece of terrific news.
- Say something provocative or challenging.
- Give a short list of hard facts or statistics if you know there are a lot of left-brain thinkers in the audience.
- Ask a question and get people in the audience involved by demanding answers or some other participation.
- If you can do it well, tell a joke.
- Tell a story. A spellbinding story that enchants your listeners is a wonderful way to involve the audience without putting them on the spot. Practice beforehand so that you can do it well.

Into the Meat of Your Presentation

Speak with energy and enthusiasm. If you feel passionately about your topic, your audience will catch your enthusiasm and get involved. Positive energy from the audience is the most wonderful reward you can have for taking the time and trouble to overcome your fears and get into public speaking.

Be aware of the audience. Notice if people are getting fidgety or looking at their watches and bring things to a close sooner rather than later. Timing your talk beforehand will ensure that you do not talk too long. Few people mind if you are briefer than expected, but they will resent your going too long.

Make notes of things you want to change, stress, eliminate or check up on before leaving for the day. Use feedback from others to help you do better next time, remembering not to take it personally or let it get you down. The critics would almost certainly do no better in your shoes. If you have promised more information to individuals in the audience, make sure you follow through.

Be Smart — Share the Load

- Today, there is a wealth of technical aids for presentations. If you're uncomfortable in front of an audience, use visual equipment to talk for you.

- Make it a joint venture. Share the presentation with a colleague or two.

- Ask people in the audience who you know have expertise in one of the areas your talk touches on to add a few words. Let them know beforehand if you don't want to put them on the spot and to be sure that your points of view are compatible!

Your Speaking Style

Just as we have different personalities and ways of handling other aspects of our lives, so our speaking styles differ also. Knowing your style and making it work for you is a good idea since we are most comfortable and convincing when acting naturally. We can, with practice and experience, vary our primary style and make ourselves more valuable to our audience by adopting from other styles that might suit that audience better.

People generally tend to be either introverts who have more trouble with speaking in public, especially if they are shy, or extroverts who will be better at hiding their nervousness and less worried about making themselves look foolish.

Some people are more organized than others. They are good at getting their speech in order and the facts told. Less organized people will need to work on the structure of their talk. They will need to watch that they do not get off topic or talk too long.

Dynamic Presentations

People who relate well to others and who have open, friendly natures have less trouble getting audiences to participate and relax. Those who are not good at forming relationships will need to work at ways to make people willing to listen.

Confidence in speaking to a group, no matter how small or how large, will only come with time and practice.

REFLECTIONS

Reflections on Making Dynamic Presentations

Take the Talk Test. Answer true or false to these presentation-giver beliefs.

Experienced presenters and born speakers never experience stage fright.	True	False
It is best not to try public speaking if you are nervous.	True	False
Keep your eyes on your notes and avoid eye contact to keep from being nervous.	True	False
You don't need presenting skills for meetings or training staff.	True	False
When people are not paying attention, you should raise your voice.	True	False
Avoid humor.	True	False
Leave the use of aids and equipment to people who know how to use them.	True	False
Put the whole thing out of your mind once it is over, give yourself a pat on the back and forget it.	True	False

All of the above statements are false.

9 THE NEXT STEP

> *"Words are indeed a mighty tool, our most precious and powerful commodity."*
> — Whoopi Goldberg

Messages bounce off the moon and space probes land on Mars, yet talking is still troublesome for us. Human cooperation and understanding come only through verbal communication. But so do conflict, cruelty and misunderstanding. Communication is the cornerstone of every relationship. When open, clear communication takes place, the relationship flourishes. When communication is blocked or muddled, the relationship suffers accordingly. In fact, psychologist Carl Rogers defines the practice of psychotherapy as the process of dealing with the failures of communication.

The success of an organization depends upon the communication skills of all employees. When 170 corporations were asked their primary reason for rejecting an applicant, "inability to communicate" and "poor communication skills" were mentioned most frequently. People who understand how communication functions in a business have a wide repertoire of written and oral communication skills and know when and how to use these skills to advance more rapidly and contribute more fully to their organizations.

The Good News Gets Better

As a professional woman today, you already know that there are vast changes in the role of women in business.

DYNAMIC COMMUNICATION SKILLS FOR WOMEN

At the dawn of the new millennium, women constitute 52 percent of the population. We are the majority, and it is time to start thinking and acting that way.

- Women hold more middle-management and supervisory jobs in North American companies than men.

- Among heterosexual couples, females more often earn more than their male partners.

- More companies than ever are coming into line with the concept of equal pay for work of equal value.

- More women than men are taking university classes and graduating from all types of institutes of higher learning. The old excuse that there are no suitably educated women for higher status jobs is no longer valid.

- Older women are coming back into the work force in larger numbers than are older men.

- More than one-third of small-business entrepreneurs in the United States are women.

- Women entrepreneurs are less likely to go bankrupt than men.

- Professions that were once male-dominated, such as accounting, medicine and law, have all become 30 percent to 50 percent feminine in the last quarter of the 20th century.

- More publications concerning business are produced for and by women, and more women than men read such materials and attend training seminars.

- Women are much more likely than men to use networking and form cordial business relations.

- Women starting out are more likely to choose a female mentor to help them get a start and avoid errors.

THE NEXT STEP

Some Imperfections Remain

- Life is still difficult for women with less education, no skills or who use poor English.

- Women of color are still noticeably confined to low-paid, unskilled jobs.

- Many older women have no pension plan or benefits.

- Young women with no high school diploma often have to work two or more part-time jobs without benefits, yet make barely enough to live on.

- Good day care is hard to find and is expensive for single-income families.

- Some companies cling to old-fashioned, hierarchical, rigid structures that do not accommodate the special needs of working women.

- Many women are caught in the sandwich generation, looking after children or grandchildren plus elderly parents, as well as holding down a job.

- Many women lose status or pension benefits if they are forced to quit work to look after elders.

- Sexual abuse, harassment and violence against women are still major societal problems.

- Stereotypes are not easily overcome.

- Women still have to try harder to be better to get the credit they deserve.

- The glass ceiling is still in position in many companies. They talk the talk but do not walk the walk when it comes to equal opportunity in the workplace. Women's skills are often less valued than those of men.

Dynamic Communication Skills for Women

- Men have had the top status jobs for a long time; they might resent losing power and find ways to take out that resentment on female employees.

- Business language and rules tend to be made for and by men. Women have to know the rules before they can play the game successfully and start making their own rules.

Building Your Edge

Language is power. It grants admittance to or exclusion from many fields. Becoming an effective communicator is your edge, your personal power base that moves you well up and beyond the glass ceiling.

Improving your communication power and confidence is possible through a concerted, conscientious effort. The question is where to apply the effort? What are your goals? What are your strengths as a communicator? What areas do you need to concentrate your time and effort on?

Only you can make the decision to improve your personal situation, no matter:

- What your present status
- The level of education you have reached so far
- The color of your skin
- Your length of time in this country
- Your economic situation
- Where you live and work

YOU are the one who can change things if you want to try.

It has been said that about 60 percent of the population believes that they will win the lottery and live happily ever after. The chances of winning millions are small, less than the chance of being struck by lightning, twice! Not

THE NEXT STEP

only that, studies show that lottery winners not only suffer from almost overwhelming levels of stress, but they seldom manage their money well either. Most end up giving the stuff away to friends and relatives and blowing large sums on foolish things.

Learn to take responsibility for yourself. Decide today to begin making and reaching goals that will enable you to become a truly dynamic person.

The Final Word

This summing-up chapter began with a quote from Whoopi Goldberg. "Words are indeed a mighty tool, our most precious and powerful commodity." Take her words to heart as you start to find ways to express yourself with more honesty and clarity.

Psychologist Carl Rogers said that effective communication requires three essential qualities:

1. Genuineness — being honest and open about feelings, needs and ideas.

2. Nonpossessive love — accepting, respecting and supporting another person in a nonpaternalistic and freeing way.

3. Empathy — the ability to see and hear another person's perspective.

Communication flows out of these basic attitudes as well as through specific methods and techniques. Communication techniques are useful to facilitate the expression of essential human qualities. The person who masters the skills of communication but lacks love and empathy will find her expertise ineffective. Important as they are, communication techniques by themselves will not produce satisfactory relationships.

You don't have to talk like a man to get ahead. Talk like a woman who intends to make this a world where women and men can work together in partnership, with dignity and equality for all.

Dynamic Communication Skills for Women

- Know your values and where you want to go.

- Believe in yourself and your ability to learn enough to keep your values and still get to the top.

- Know what you want yourself and make sure that others understand you when you speak.

- Present the professional, dynamic, assertive image that you want others to have of you.

REFLECTIONS

1. Choosing Role Models

Choose someone you believe to be a successful communicator to be your role model. Preferably choose another woman.

Watch and analyze her communication:

- Why is it effective?

- How does she express her views?

- How does she handle anger?

- How does she give and receive compliments?

- How does she give and receive criticism?

- What is her personal style?

Measure your communication skills against hers. What can you learn from her? What can you adapt from her style?

Reflections

REFLECTIONS

2. Setting Goals

Form your first goal.

Perhaps you discovered where you want to begin during one of the earlier reflection page exercises in this book? Perhaps your determination to begin to change came from something you read in one of the chapters? Possibly you were led to read or study some of the suggested materials? Maybe the last exercise or one of the inspiring quotes got you thinking?

Whatever the reason for your resolution to start making changes in your life, act now. If you put it off, you will slip back into apathy again, and valuable time will be lost.

Use the space below. Think in terms of "stop doing" and "start doing."

Remember:
- Keep your goals short and achievable.
- Give yourself enough time.
- Do not give up if you don't succeed at first.
- Compose some positive self-talk statements that you can use daily to encourage yourself as you go.
- Know and use your current skills and abilities to help you reach your goals.
- Use the tips and ideas in this book as well as other suggested material to help you reach your goal.
- Involve a friend or mentor who will help you make it through.
- Visualize yourself reaching your goal.
- Reward yourself for each step you achieve.

REFLECTIONS

List four goals, why you want to achieve them, when you want to achieve them, and the first step you will take to achieve them.

1. **Goal:**

    Why:

    When:

    Action:

2. **Goal:**

    Why:

    When:

    Action:

3. **Goal:**

    Why:

    When:

    Action:

4. **Goal:**

    Why:

    When:

    Action:

INDEX

A
active listening   34, 36, 38
adjectives   5-6, 10, 14
adverbs   5
aggression   15, 19-22, 28-29, 36, 44, 53, 57, 63, 67-68, 71
aggressive reaction   15
apologizing   6-7, 16, 41, 63, 101
asking the right question   34
assertive
   behavior   20, 67-68, 74-75
   body language   48, 57
   communication   19, 21-31
   message   25
   template   25, 31
assertiveness   3, 15, 22, 29, 43, 98-99, 118
   steps to   22
assessments   72, 89
attention, getting   37, 46, 59, 98, 108

B
body language   10, 34, 36, 40-41, 43-44, 47-48, 53-58
business conflicts   61, 69

C

call-waiting   97
Carr-Ruffino, Norma   74
Coleman, Daniel   35-36
combatants
    the accommodator   63
    the avoider   62-63
    the competitor   63
    the compromiser   64
    the negotiator   64
competition   11, 64
compliments   61, 77-80, 82-83, 86, 119
conflict   3, 25, 61-69, 83, 113
confrontation   28, 68, 77
crisis   61, 69-72, 83-84, 89
crisis management   70-71, 84
criticism   23, 61, 72-77, 83, 85, 119

D

delegating   4, 26
documentation   80, 88-89
dress choice   52
dress code   52
dynamic energy   80

E

e-mail   5, 25, 87
empathy   35, 68, 117
effective communicator   116
effective writing   87-96
emotions   14-15, 65, 68, 76
evaluations   72-73, 89
eye contact   34, 40-41, 47-48, 57, 59, 107, 112

INDEX

F
feedback   9, 72-77, 110
   on performance   72-73
feeling guilty   26
frankness   15

G
gender differences   3, 9, 12, 16
generalizations   12
genuineness   117
glass ceiling   115-116
Goldberg, Whoopi   113, 117
gossip   13, 15, 70
grammar   90, 95-96

H
habits of speech   3
honest feedback   76

I
I-message   23-28, 30-31, 36, 54, 79, 83-86
inflection   4, 16
intuition, women's   36

K
knowing your subject   89, 104
knowing your audience   90-91, 94, 96, 100, 105, 109

L
leadership qualities   3, 29
learning from criticism   75
linear thinking   15
listening   3, 8-9, 14, 21, 23, 33-41, 47, 57, 65-66, 68, 73, 75, 81, 93, 97,
         105, 107-109, 111
logical evaluation   75

M
Malloy, John   54-55
memos   5, 88

N
negative self-talk   23, 81-82
nonassertiveness   21
nonpossessive love   117
nonverbal input   9
nonverbals   43-59
   types of:
      give me some space   48
      I don't get any respect around here   50
      I hate those limp handshakes   50
      look 'em square in the eye   47
      masterful tone   45
      poker face   45
      stand up for yourself   53
      the right suit won't get you in the boardroom, but the wrong one will keep you out   52

O
objective words   14

P
passivity   19-20, 22, 53
personal interactions   24
personal space   48, 57
perspective   19, 74-75, 117
politeness   13-15
positive self-talk   80-82, 108, 120
posture   34, 43-44, 53-55, 57, 59, 106
preparation pointers   106-108
presentations   103-105, 107, 109-112
problem-solving   8, 27, 29, 36, 68

INDEX

professional image   5
pruning sentences   14, 90
public speaking   47, 103-104, 109, 112

Q
quick quiz   2

R
reflections   16-17, 31, 40-41, 59, 83-86, 96, 102, 112, 119-121
respect   20-21, 26, 29-30, 50, 55, 58, 63, 65, 67, 70, 75, 81
responsibility   7-8, 16, 26, 29, 72, 74, 117
Rogers, Carl   113, 117
rudeness   15

S
saying no   26-27, 38
self-confidence   3, 28, 52
self-esteem   15, 20, 23, 47, 62, 69, 72, 74-75, 81, 86, 99, 104
sexual harassment   79-80
silence   3, 6, 9, 14, 53, 67, 72, 97
speaking style, masculine   10
spell check   90, 95
status symbols   50
stereotypes   13-14, 115
stress   20, 52-53, 99, 103, 110, 117

T
taking criticism   74-75
Tannen, Deborah   11-13
technical aids   110
telephone battle   98-99
telephone negatives   97
telephone usage, thirty tips for   99-101
Twain, Mark   80
team leader   29

temptation to blame   30

U
unwritten message   91

V
visual aids   105-106

W
winning   11, 99, 116
words, choice of   10
writing   5, 14, 24, 87-96

Buy any 3, get 1 FREE!

BUY 3 GET 1 FREE! Buy more, save more!

Get a 60-Minute Training Series™ Handbook FREE ($14.95 value)* when you buy any three. See back of order form for full selection of titles.

These are helpful how-to books for you, your employees and co-workers. Add to your library. Use for new-employee training, brown-bag seminars, promotion gifts and more. Choose from many popular titles on a variety of lifestyle, communication, productivity and leadership topics. Exclusively from National Press Publications.

DESKTOP HANDBOOK ORDER FORM

Ordering is easy:

1. Complete both sides of this Order Form, detach, and mail, fax or phone your order to:

   Mail: National Press Publications
   P.O. Box 419107
   Kansas City, MO 64141-6107

   Fax: 1-913-432-0824
   Phone: 1-800-258-7248 (in Canada 1-800-685-4142)
   Internet: http://www.natsem.com/books.html

2. Please print:

   Name_____ Position/Title _____
   Company/Organization_____
   Address_____City _____
   State/Province_____ZIP/Postal Code _____
   Telephone (____)_____ Fax (____)_____
   E-Mail_____

3. Easy payment:
   ❏ Enclosed is my check or money order for $_____ (total from back).
   Please make payable to National Press Publications.

   Please charge to:
   ❏ MasterCard   ❏ VISA   ❏ American Express
   Credit Card No. _____ Exp. Date_____
   Signature_____

   •

   ### MORE WAYS TO SAVE:

   SAVE 33%!!! BUY 20-50 COPIES of any title ... pay just $9.95 each ($11.25 Canadian).
   SAVE 40%!!! BUY 51 COPIES OR MORE of any title ... pay just $8.95 each ($10.25 Canadian).

   * $20.00 in Canada

VIP No. 922-008438-099   8/00

Buy 3, get 1 FREE!
60-MINUTE TRAINING SERIES™ HANDBOOKS

TITLE	RETAIL PRICE	QTY	TOTAL
8 Steps for Highly Effective Negotiations #424	$14.95		
Assertiveness #4422	$14.95		
Balancing Career and Family #415	$14.95		
Delegate for Results #4592	$14.95		
Dynamic Communication Skills for Women #4309	$14.95		
The Essentials of Business Writing #4310	$14.95		
Exceptional Customer Service #4882	$14.95		
Fear & Anger: Slay the Dragons … #4302	$14.95		
Getting Things Done #4112	$14.95		
How to Coach an Effective Team #4308	$14.95		
How to De-Junk Your Life #4306	$14.95		
How to Handle Conflict and Confrontation #4952	$14.95		
How to Manage Your Boss #493	$14.95		
How to Supervise People #4102	$14.95		
How to Work With People #4032	$14.95		
Inspire & Motivate Through Performance Reviews #4232	$14.95		
Listen Up: Hear What's Really Being Said #4172	$14.95		
Motivation and Goal-Setting #4962	$14.95		
A New Attitude #4432	$14.95		
Parenting: Ward & June … #486	$14.95		
The Polished Professional #4262	$14.95		
The Power of Innovative Thinking #428	$14.95		
The Power of Self-Managed Teams #4222	$14.95		
Powerful Communication Skills #4132	$14.95		
Present With Confidence #4612	$14.95		
The Secret to Developing Peak Performers #4692	$14.95		
Self-Esteem: The Power to Be Your Best #4642	$14.95		
Shortcuts to Organized Files & Records #4307	$14.95		
The Stress Management Handbook #4842	$14.95		
Supreme Teams: How to Make Teams Work #4303	$14.95		
Thriving on Change #4212	$14.95		
Women and Leadership #4632	$14.95		

Sales Tax
All purchases subject to state and local sales tax.
Questions?
Call
1-800-258-7248

Subtotal	$
Add 7% Sales Tax (Or add appropriate state and local tax)	$
Shipping and Handling ($3 one item; 50¢ each additional item)	$
TOTAL	$